Contents

Foreword

Why Grammar, Spelling and Punctuation Matter in the Internet Age

Let me confess my vested interest. I am a freelance training consultant, and a lot of my work revolves around business and legal writing skills. I am probably biased therefore in wanting people to want to learn about grammar, sentence construction and so on. I started out life as a practising lawyer, where accuracy is of paramount importance in the drafting of legal documents. I also run courses for other business organisations such as banks, accountancy firms and insurance companies where senior managers have asked me to address problems like: grammatical howlers in correspondence, verbose and repetitive reports, inappropriate use of slang and emoticons in emails etc.

But in recent years I have become more and more disturbed by press and news articles on the rise of shorthand language in SMS messages, posts on Twitter and suchlike; and I began to wonder if I was facing obsolescence in my work and if I should find another area to concentrate on. However, one day in 2011 I saw an article on the BBC News website in which an online entrepreneur said that, in his opinion, poor spelling could cut online sales in half through customers being put off or thinking that a poorly spelled website was bogus. This view was then echoed by the Confederation of British Industry, one of whose members reported a 100% increase in sales from a website after correcting a glaring spelling error. In fact the working title for this book was "Wrong Wrong Wrong" following the complaints I have received from managers about their staffs' writing – but I though this might be a tad negative!

This got me thinking, since of course Internet commerce relies so much on the written word. Shortly after reading the BBC website feature I booked a parking space at a private car park near to Heathrow Airport, and as usual I then printed off the travel directions. There was a small, sketchy map which was next to useless, but fortunately there was a paragraph of street-by-street directions on how to get there from the M4 motorway.

We almost missed our flight. The website's written directions were so garbled and unintelligible, the place was almost impossible to find. Fortunately we had a large London A to Z in the car which just about stretched to this obscure pocket of Hounslow, and we managed to get to Heathrow Airport in time to catch our flight. I swore never to use the company again after our collective nervous breakdown thanks to their poorly written website, even though we now know where the wretched car park is.

So that was the inspiration for this book. There are many excellent grammar books on the market, and similarly there are lots of writing style guides. This book attempts to deal with both of these areas, providing a comprehensive grammar handy with some tips on how to write economically and accurately. Whether you are designing a website, blogging, tweeting, composing an email or writing a document to go as an email attachment, this book will give you the tools to do so with clarity and confidence.

I hope you enjoy reading it and that you will find it useful as a reference work in your desk drawer. The worked examples of business documents are not intended to be prescriptive but they do (I hope) follow best practice.

Many thanks to the City Careers Series editor Jake Schogger, without whose faith and perseverance this book would not have been possible. Thanks also to Chris Phillips (www.cphillipsdesign.uk) for his fantastic graphic design work throughout (and endless patience with Jake Schogger).

John Trimbos

London 2016

Introduction

The main part of this book consists of an ABC of pithy guidance about grammar, spelling, punctuation and writing style. If you follow these guidelines you will not go far wrong. But let us start with some pitfalls to avoid – the Seven Deadly Sins which too many people commit too often.

1. Writing for yourself rather than for the reader

Here is an example of a press release issued by a major car manufacturer:

"The selection of materials for the A-Class is based on scientific studies conducted in the laboratories of XXXXXXXX's research department. Motorists assessed the touch and feel of a range of different materials, switches and controls, and were able to provide valuable pointers for the development of interior components which not only look good but are also pleasant to the touch."

What they meant was:

"If you sit in our new A-Class, you will notice lots of attractive soft-touch plastics."

Moral: focus on the benefit to the reader rather than banging your corporate drum.

2. Putting up barriers between you and your readership

How does the following sound?

"The firm's policies and procedures are contained in the new staff handbook; additionally some insights into our main clients have been provided. It is recommended that, after studying the handbook, any areas of activity which are not fully understood should be discussed with your manager."

That is pretty cold and impersonal. If you use words like "you" and "your", you speak directly to the reader, which is just as professional but much warmer and more accessible:

"Our new staff handbook contains all of the firm's policies and procedures, together with some insights into our main clients. If you have any queries, please discuss them with your manager."

3. Failing to observe ABC (Accuracy, Brevity, Clarity)

This is a letter written by a partner in a top 20 City law firm:

"We recently wrote to you in order to provide you with an application for a subscription to your publication. We do not appear to have received a copy of the same from you or an acknowledgment of our application, and should be grateful to hear from you in this respect with an acknowledgment of our application and confirmation of when we may hear from you with a copy of the latest issue."

The second sentence is 52 words long! The whole letter ought to be shorter than this:

"We recently sent you a subscription to your publication but have heard nothing. Please acknowledge safe receipt and let us know when we will receive our first issue."

4. Failing to write for a global audience

If you are writing for the web, or if you are sending emails across the world, remember not to use too many colloquialisms which may not translate well. People on the other side of the world may not appreciate why an idea might be "too ivory tower" or "pie in the sky", or why a project should "wash its own face". Use a plain English alternative instead: "too academic", or the project should not make a loss.

5. Using too many abbreviations or jargon

How many Americans know what HMRC is? Or how many British people know what the IRS is? They are equivalent organisations on both sides of the Atlantic: Her Majesty's Revenue and Customs and the Inland Revenue Service.

Organisations often have their own shorthand which may not travel well. An old boss of mine once received an email from his senior partner who was under the mistaken impression that it was cool to use SMS shorthand in emails. It read as follows: "UR CRP". My boss was initially very offended and was about to write back, "UR SHT" or UR WNKR", when he remembered that C.R.P. was the firm's shorthand for "client relationship partner" (i.e. it was a really nice email saying that a new client was his responsibility).

6. Using too many hyperlinks

Putting too many hyperlinks on your website or in an email will tend to take people away from you and to somewhere/someone else. Make sure that any hyperlinks open up in a new window, and if possible group hyperlinks in one place such as the bottom of the page.

7. Failing to proof read and check the finished work

Probably the worst typo to appear in print was Penguin's "The Pasta Bible" published in 2010. It was rapidly recalled when it was pointed out that one recipe, instead of specifying "freshly ground black pepper", called for "freshly ground black people". Heaven only knows what the proof reader was thinking of...

Grammar, Spelling and Punctuation

A lot of people tell me that they have unresolved issues about grammar, sentence construction and so on. This chapter is designed to clarify some of the knottiest problems encountered in business writing, and also to address some myths promulgated by some members of the teaching profession in our schools.

Chapter 1: Back To Basics (...just for a moment)

Time to dispel some myths and misconceptions

There are many writing myths which seem to be drummed into people at school. The most common, which I am asked about almost every week, is why it is unacceptable to put "and" before a comma. It is not unacceptable at all. There is only one comma which we do not generally put before "and" - this is the so-called Victorian or Oxford comma, which can appear in lists:

"We bought pens, pencils, paper, rubbers and rulers."

If I had put another comma before "and rulers" in the above example then this would have been the Oxford comma. It would not be wrong to put it before the "and" – it is simply reckoned to look old-fashioned. If you have a series of phrases rather than just individual nouns, then the Victorian or Oxford comma may still be useful to clarify your meaning:

"We should not forget the various crisps for the picnic: beef and mustard, cheese and onion, red chilli, and salt and vinegar."

The four most common writing myths

1. **You must not put a comma before "and".** Of course we know that you *can*, but if you do not believe me here is the first line of George Orwell's *1984*: "It was a bright cold day in April, and all the clocks were striking thirteen."

2. **You must not end a sentence with a preposition.** Winston Churchill illustrated the absurdity of this supposed rule during World War II when he was plagued by a civil servant who wrote grammatically perfect but almost unintelligible memos to him. In the margin of one memo he wrote: "This is the kind of language up with which I cannot put." No one should ever write like that, so by all means end the sentence with a preposition: "This is the kind of language I cannot put up *with*."

3. **You must not start a sentence with "but".** But you can. Here is a sentence from Jane Austen's *Mansfield Park* in a paragraph describing the heroine and her sisters: "But there certainly are not so many men of large fortune in the world, as there are pretty women to deserve them."

4. **You must not split the infinitive.** The infinitive or basic version of a verb is always two words: "to write", "to speak" "to be or not to be" etc. Many people frown upon splitting the infinitive (i.e. inserting another word in-between: "to quickly write", "to loudly speak" etc.), instead preferring to including a descriptive word after the verb: "to write quickly", "to speak loudly" etc.). I have checked this out in a number of grammar and style guides, and they all say that it is technically correct to split the infinitive but inadvisable because so many people think it is wrong. This is probably the most famous example in recent culture, from the spoken introduction to *Star Trek*: "To *boldly* go where no one has gone before." A more highbrow example is a line of poetry by Lord Byron: "To *slowly* trace the forest's shady scene."

A little light relief...

Here is another example of a split infinitive, but I think the problem lies towards the end of the sentence:

"This being Easter Sunday, we will ask the vicar's wife to slowly walk up the aisle and lay an egg on the altar."

Subjects, objects and articles for the unwary

A lot of people now seem to disregard the rules about "who" and "whom"; "me" and "I"; and "a", "an" and "the", but I think this is dangerous. Certainly in business writing we should observe these rules strictly. This section will therefore seek to clarify them once and for all.

"I" or "me"

What would you write here? "Amber went to the meeting with Colin and I/me?"

The answer is "me" because "I" goes with the subject ("I am going...") whereas "me" goes with the object ("Come with me"). There is however a neat trick you can play here to help you choose the right word, which is to get rid of the other person. In this case get rid of Colin and what would you say? "Amber went to the meeting with me" – not "Amber went to the meeting with I".

"Who" or "whom"

The rule here is that "who" goes with the subject and "whom" goes with the object. In the below statement, the *secretary* performs the action (the *secretary* is starting next week) so she takes "who":

"The secretary who starts next week has great references."

But in the below statement, the subject is *me* because *I* performed the action (i.e. the interviewing). The *secretary* is the object in the sentence because the *secretary* received the interview from me, so she takes "whom":

"The secretary whom I interviewed has great references."

There is another trick here which will tell you the right answer. Focus on the letter "m" – whenever you would say "him" (or "her" of course, although this does not fit the "m" rule!) or "them", you should say "whom". Going back to the recruitment of the secretary above, you would not say: "I interviewed he" or "Him starts next week". You would say: "I interviewed him" (or "the secretary whom I interviewed") and "He starts next week" (or "the secretary who starts").

A little light relief...

Be careful where you put your subjects and your objects in a sentence. The following sentence makes you sound like you represent a Mafia client:

"My client has discussed your proposal to fill the canal with his elderly relatives."

I think we actually mean this: "My client has discussed with his elderly relatives your proposal to fill the canal."

"A", "an" or "the"

Finally, many people who learn English as a foreign language are confused by our use of articles (using "a", "an" or "the" before a particular word) and in particular when we leave them out. In other words, why do we say, "Unemployment has risen this month" rather than "The unemployment has risen this month"? And why do we say, "The company's profits are rising" rather than just "Company's profits are rising"?

Apparently languages like Russian have no article as such, which must make life very confusing for them. The trick is to ask whether the noun in question is countable or uncountable, i.e. whether there are several of them or whether they describe something that hangs over the whole of society and cannot be distinguished from another one.

In this way it becomes easier to see why we say, "Unemployment is rising" because unemployment sits over the whole country – there are no distinct "unemployments" which differ from each other. Similarly we would say that "Secondary infection is becoming more common" because it describes the ailment in general, although we would use the article when talking about a specific infection: "The patient's secondary infection is completely cured".

A little light relief...

A medical howler:

Lawyer: "How many autopsies have you performed on dead people?"

Witness: "All my autopsies have been performed on dead people."

Chapter 2: Punctuation

Many people come to my courses with unresolved issues about punctuation, so here is my step-by-step guide to using the most common punctuation marks. Bear in mind the following general guidelines about each of these marks:

- **Parentheses (round brackets)** gather up non-essential but nice to know information.
- **The comma** is primarily the written equivalent of a spoken pause for breath.
- **The semicolon** is halfway in strength between a comma and a full stop.
- **The colon** is usually the written equivalent of an usher – it introduces things.
- **Apostrophes** show ownership and missing letters.
- **Quotation marks** are used to reproduce spoken words of text, or to give a special meaning to a word of phrase.
- **Dashes** give emphasis.
- **Hyphens** should not be confused with dashes; hyphens join words and expressions together and (unlike dashes) do not have gaps around them

Parentheses

We use these to de-emphasise non-essential material, although using two commas instead of the brackets is probably more modern:

> "Three directors (all under 45) will speak about their successful careers with their firms."

Commas

The comma is primarily the written equivalent of a spoken pause for breath.

1. Use a comma in a sentence where two complete thoughts are separated by words like "but", "or", "yet", "so", "for", "or", "and":

> "We believe you have good ideas, and the conference committee should incorporate several of them."

2. Following an introductory dependent clause:

> "Before we can launch our new courses, we need additional funds."

3. When three or more items are listed in a series:

> "We bought books, pens, pencils and printer cartridges."

4. Between consecutive adjectives where the comma is really used instead of "and":

> "Michelle hated the dark, gloomy pantry."

5. To set off parenthetical information, when it is more modern to use two commas:

> "Lionel, our HR manager, will help you complete the induction form."

6. In emails to set off the name of anyone you are addressing directly:

> "Let's end this report, Hilary, with the evaluation forms."

Semicolons

The semicolon is halfway in strength between a comma and a full stop.

1. Use a semicolon when a coordinating conjunction ("but", "or", "yet" etc.) is omitted between two complete thoughts:

   > "The finance department approved the expenditure; the marketing department disapproved."

2. Use a semicolon when two complete thoughts are linked by a transitional expression such as however or therefore:

   > "The manager has agreed to the project; however, we must await budget approval."

3. Use to separate a series of phrases that already contain commas:

   > "The board members went to different countries: David Bailey, England; Angela Knight, France; and Marcia Green, Germany."

Colons

The colon is usually the written equivalent of an usher – it introduces things.

1. Use a colon to introduce a list:

   > "Our usual training aids include the following: flip charts, Post-it notes and markers."

2. Use to separate the title from the subtitle of a book or report:

   > "Learning Styles: Everything you wanted to know about training but were afraid to ask."

3. Use to represent the word "to" in a ratio:

   > "10:1"

Apostrophes

Apostrophes show ownership and missing letters.

1. To show that one or more letters have been omitted:

   > "I can't do the report by Friday."

2. To show ownership, an "s" with an apostrophe immediately before it shows that the owner is singular:

   > "The computer's hard disc is broken."

3. An "s" with an apostrophe immediately after it shows that there is more than one owner:

   > "The twins' hairstyles were different."

   But note the exception for words that are plural but do not end in "s":

   > "The oxen's stable."

4. Use an apostrophe when the owner's name ends in an "s" and you do not want to use another "s" (the example below is reckoned to be more modern):

   > "Sian Williams' computer."

Quotation Marks

Quotation marks are used to reproduce spoken words of text, or to give a special meaning to a word of phrase.

1. To indicate the exact words of a speaker:

 John said, "All employees must attend the safety meeting tomorrow."

2. To indicate words or phrases introduced by expressions such as "labelled" or "marked":

 The box was labelled "This Side Up".

3. For direct speech, full stops, commas, colons and semicolons go inside quotation marks:

 She said, "All the reports must be in by Friday – don't let me down."

4. Question marks and exclamation marks can go either inside or outside the quotation marks:

 He asked, "How are you?" But: when will you stop saying, "No problem"?

5. If you use quotation marks, start with upper or lower case depending on what the quote starts with. In example 1 above the word "All" starts with a capital A because it is the start of the speaker's sentence. But if we fade in part way through a sentence, then the quotation starts with a small letter and is typically preceded by an ellipsis ("..."):

 He said that all staff members were "...absolutely and utterly required to attend the meeting."

6. There is no real distinction between single quotation marks ('like this') and double quotation marks ("like this"). General practice is to use double quotation marks as the default setting and to use single marks to differentiate a quotation within a quotation:

 He said, "My wife called out, 'Where are you hiding?'"

Dashes

Dashes give emphasis to particular parts of sentences.

1. Dashes can show emphasis, indicate abrupt change, or set off explanatory material instead of parentheses or commas:

 "We should determine - before the year ends - the cost of relocating the London office."

2. Dashes can be used to emphasise words or phrases at the beginning or end of a sentence:

 "Children – they are nothing but trouble and expense!"

 "This will be a long and difficult project – so be very careful."

Hyphens

Hyphens should not be confused with dashes; hyphens join words and expressions together and (unlike dashes) do not have gaps around them.

1. Hyphens are generally used for relations:

 "Mother-in-law".

2. Hyphens can clarify certain expressions:

 "in-house facilities"

3. Hyphens may also be necessary to clarify things like numbers:

   "Please order two eight-file cabinets for my office."

4. Hyphens can also help to clarify the meaning that you intend a particular phrase to have:

   "Basingstoke has little-town charm"

   ...suggests Basingstoke is a nice place to visit, whereas removing the hyphen suggests quite the opposite: "Basingstoke has little town charm".

   "I have added an extra section to your report. Please re-sign."

   ...asks the reader to sign the report again. However, removing the hyphen creates a very different effect: "I have added an extra section to your report. Please resign." This means the report was such rubbish that the reader should look for new employment.

A little light relief...

Commas in particular are quite discretionary in English, so their position can often change the meaning of a sentence by mistake. I often have fun with this unpunctuated sentence:

"Woman without her man is useless."

If I ask a mixed class to punctuate it the men tend to write:

"Woman, without her man, is useless."

Whereas the women tend to favour:

"Woman – without her, *man* is useless."

Another example is a BBC press release issued a few years ago: "By train, plane and sedan chair, Peter Ustinov retraces a journey made by Mark Twain a century ago. The highlights of his global tour include encounters with Nelson Mandela, an 800-year-old demi-god and a dildo collector."

An Oxford comma before the final "and" would have prevented Nelson Mandela being a dildo collector, although he would arguably still have been an 800 year-old demi-god. There is only so much that a mere comma can do.

Chapter 3: Grammar

People often ask me to explain terms like “pronoun” and “preposition”. Here is a guide to grammar terms so you never need to ask someone like me again.

Adjective: A word that describes a noun – “thick”, “narrow”, “green”, “mischievous”:

“The *mischievous* baby was asleep in his cot.”

Adverb: A word that gives more information about a verb – “occasionally”, “quickly”, “slowly”, “noisily”:

“The children played *noisily* in the garden.”

Adverbs can also add to or modify an adjective that immediately follows:

“John is *terribly* clever (or egotistical)”; “It is *extremely* cold in here”.

Clause: A group of words that includes a verb and forms part of a sentence. An independent clause expresses a complete thought and can stand alone as a sentence. A dependent clause does not express a complete thought and cannot stand alone as a sentence.

Conjunction: A connecting word –“and”, “as”, “or”, “but”, “since”, “when”:

“The plane had just landed *when* the brakes failed.”

Interjection: Expresses exclamation – “Help!”:

“Ouch! That hurt!” she shouted.

Modifier: A word, clause or phrase that qualifies the meaning of a word; adjectives, adverbs and descriptive phrases are all examples of modifiers:

My cat, a *silver tabby*, always covers my velvet jacket with fur.”

Noun: A word that is the name of a person, place or thing:

“bicycle”, “house”, “accountant”

Object: Whatever follows and receives the action of the verb:

“We purchased a *computer*.”

Predicate: Provides information about the subject (“Helen” being the subject in the below example):

“Helen writes excellent business reports.”

Preposition: A word that expresses the relationship between a noun and some other part of the same sentence – “to”, “at”, “by”, “from” – do:

“The paper is next to the printer.”

Pronoun: Takes the place of a noun – “he”, “she”,” it”, “me”, “them”:

“John said that he did it.”

Sentence: A group of words comprising a subject and a verb that states a complete concept or idea.

Subject: the actor within the sentence:

“The *forensic accountant* examined the report.”

Verb: A word that expresses an action:

“My children *walk* to school every morning.”

A verb can also indicate a state of mind:

“The matron *thought* she could hear noises in the basement.”

A little light relief...

Be careful with your prepositions. This was seen in a church parish newsletter:

“Remember in prayer the many who are sick of our church and community.”

Of course, the church actually meant: “Remember in prayer the many who are sick *within* our church and community.”

Chapter 4: Commonly Misspelled, Dangerous and Tricky Words

There are various words that a lot of people repeatedly spell or use incorrectly. This chapter provides a quick reference guide that aims to ensure that *you* are no longer one of the many.

The 150 most commonly misspelled words

Apparently these are the 150 most commonly misspelled words in English (they are written in UK English):

A	**Absence** **Acceptable** **Accommodate** **Accuracy** **Acquaint** **Acquire** **Adapt** **Adequately** **Adolescent** **Advertise** **Adviser** (**"advisor"** in American English, which is increasingly seen here too so either is now fine in UK English) **Affect**	**All right** **Amateur** **Among** **Analyse** **Annually** **Apparent** **Appearance** **Argument** **Athletic** **Attendance** **Auxiliary** **Awkward** **Aggravate**
B	**Battery** **Beginning**	**Beneficiary** **Bureaucracy**
C	**Calendar** **Carefully** **Catalogue** **Cemetery** **Chief**	**Commitment** **Committee** **Controlled** **Criticised**
D	**Definitely** **Description** **Develop** **Difference** **Disappear**	**Disappoint** **Disapprove** **Discussion** **Dividend** **Division**
E	**Effect** **Embarrassed** **Exaggerate**	**Excellent** **Expense**
F	**Facsimile** **Fascinate** **February** **Finally**	**Financially** **Forty** **Fulfil**
G	**Government** **Governor**	**Guarantee**
H	**Humorous**	
I	**Illogical** **Imaginary** **Immediately** **Inconvenience** **Independent** **Indispensable**	**Inoculate** **Interest** **Interruption** **Invariably** **Irresistible**

J	**Jewellery**	**Judgement** (or **"judgment"** if referring to a judgment of a UK or European court)
K	**Knowledgeable**	
L	**Laboratory** **Latter** **Leisurely**	**Liaise** **License/licence** **Lonely**
M	**Maintenance** **Manoeuvre** **Maybe**	**Meant** **Mortgage**
N	**Necessary** **Nickel** **Ninety**	**Noticeable** **Nuclear** **Nuisance**
O	**Occasion** **Occurrence**	**Occurring** **Oppressed**
P	**Parallel** **Particle** **Pastime** **Possibly** **Practically** **Precede** **Precedent**	**Preference** **Privilege** **Probably** **Proceed** **Pronunciation** **Propaganda** **Proposal**
Q	**Questionnaire**	
R	**Receive** **Recommend** **Responsibility**	**Responsible** **Restaurant** **Rhythm**
S	**Satellite** **Secretary** **Seize** **Separate** **Signature** **Sincerely** **Skiing** **Souvenir**	**Strictly** **Stubbornness** **Succeed** **Success** **Summarised** **Superintendent** **Surprise** **Swimming**
T	**Tendency** **Therefore** **Thorough**	**Through** **Transferred** **Truly**
U	**Unanimous** **Until**	**Used to** **Usually**
V	**Vacuum** **Vertical**	**Vitamin**
W	**Weird**	

Spell checker will pick most of these up, but if you have a blind spot for any then it is a good idea to familiarise yourself with them.

American English

For completeness we should add a note about differences in American English.

-re or -er

UK English spells a lot of words with –re (centre, fibre, litre, theatre) that Americans spell with –er. There are exceptions though, which are spelled with –re on both sides of the Atlantic: acre, mediocre, massacre etc.

-ise or -ize

The Oxford English Dictionary recognises both spellings but in the UK we tend to favour –ise for words like organise, criticise and realise. In America they replace with "s" with a "z" in most cases, but not for: advertise, advise, comprise, compromise, devise, excise, franchise, improvise, incise, merchandise, revise, supervise and surprise.

-our or -or

In the UK we spell these words as follows: colour, behaviour, flavour, neighbour, honour, armour, savour, labour, rumour and humour. In America these words are spelled with –or, but some words where you pronounce the "u" are spelled with –our, such as contour and paramour.

-ce or -se

In UK English we spell advice/advise, licence/license and practice/practise differently according to whether we are talking about the noun or the verb. In America they always spell practice with a "c", and advise and license with an "s". They also spell other words with –se which we would always spell with –ce such as: defense, offense and pretense (these are the American spellings).

A little light relief...

There are also other words which simply differ on both sides of the Atlantic: autumn/fall, petrol/gas, lift/elevator, pavement/sidewalk, boot/trunk, toilet/restroom.

I have some very good American friends whom I meet in Cape Cod every few years. On one occasion we were having a barbecue and I told the other father: "You can inform the masses that my bangers are ready for consumption." He replied: "I certainly can, but I really don't know if what you're proposing is legal here or not." Note to American readers: "bangers" is slang for sausages in the UK, especially when they burst open.

Dangerous and tricky words

English has many similar sounding but misleading words, or words which are spelled a bit too similarly. I often see "disinterested" used instead of "bored" or "uninterested" in the quality press, which really is a cause for concern. I also once saw a memo from a senior partner in a City law firm using the wrong "discreet/discrete", although this may have just been a typo.

Here are the most dangerous words for you to beware of (please note that these are UK English spellings):

1. Advise/advice

"Advise" is the verb meaning to give guidance:

"I must advise you to be careful."

"Advice" is the noun, the guidance that is given:

"I should like to give you some good advice."

2. Affect/effect

"Affect" is a verb meaning to alter or to change (the best way to remember this is to focus on the letter "a"):

"An organisation's profitability can affect the level of salary increases."

"Effect" (to cause maximum confusion) can be a noun meaning an effect or a result:

"Global warming is having an increasingly strong effect on our climate."

It can also be a verb, but a different one from "affect" – as a verb it means to introduce or to cause something to happen:

"The firm has effected some new health and safety policies."

3. Among/between

"Among" is used for more than two things or people:

"He divided the money among the triplets."

"Between" is only to be used where you divide something two ways:

"He divided the money between the twins."

Note "among" and "amongst" are interchangeable, as are "while" and "whilst" – the former are more modern and preferable.

A little light relief...

An American court was recently asked to rule on the interpretation of a last will and testament. The testator left a legacy (i.e. a specific sum) to be distributed "between the nephews and nieces" of two named relations. There were twenty assorted nephews and nieces.

The executors of the estate were about to send out twenty cheques in the same amount, when one of the nephews challenged the interpretation of the will. Breeding rates differed within the family – the first relation had only one nephew (who challenged the will), whereas relation number two had nineteen assorted nephews and nieces. The nephew therefore argued that the money should be split two ways (i.e. half to him and half to the other nineteen) and the court agreed because the will used the word "between" instead of the correct "among". His name is probably mud now at family reunions, since he walked away with 50% of the legacy instead of 5%, which is probably not what the testator intended – but the nephew probably does not give a tinker's cuss, as they say.

4. Continual/continuous

"Continual" describes something that occurs with pauses and intermissions:

"The computer continually breaks down."

"Continuous" describes something that occurs without any pauses:

"The roar of the waterfall was continuous."

5. Complement/compliment

"Complement" means something that goes well with something else:

"His seriousness is the perfect complement to my humour."

"Compliments" are nice, flattering comments:

"After my gastric band operation my waistline received lots of compliments."

6. Dependent/dependant

"Dependent" is an adjective, meaning a state of depending on something:

"The agreement is dependent on satisfaction of the conditions precedent."

"Dependants" are people who depend on someone else:

"The testator wants to make ample provision for his dependants."

7. Discreet/discrete

"Discreet" means that someone is careful with information, not inclined to gossip:

"You can confide in him – he's very discreet."

"Discrete" means separate or distinct:

"If you issue proceedings in Scotland, rather than England, there are discrete processes to follow."

8. Disinterested/uninterested

"Disinterested" means impartial, showing no prejudice:

"To serve on a jury, you must be truly disinterested."

"Uninterested" means bored or lacking interest:

"He was uninterested and took no part in the meeting."

9. Eager/anxious

"Eager" means fervent or enthusiastic:

"I am eager for news about my secondment."

"Anxious" means full of worry:

"Her work colleagues were anxious about her poor health."

10. Enquiry/inquiry

"Enquiry", although technically interchangeable with "inquiry", is better used for individuals so you would write to a client:

"Thank you for your recent enquiry..."

"Inquiry" is better used for official investigations such as police inquiries into a crime or a public inquiry into an infrastructure proposal.

11. Farther/further

"Farther" refers to physical distance:

"It is farther to Glasgow from here than it is to Edinburgh."

"Further" refers to degree or extent:

"Further time is needed to complete the task."

12. Imply/infer

"Imply" is the verb meaning to throw out a hint or suggestion:

"She implied by her manner that she was unhappy with her manager."

"Infer" is the mirror of "imply", meaning to take in a hint or suggestion:

"I inferred from her manner that she was unhappy with her manager."

13. Its/it's

"Its" is the possessive pronoun, belonging to it:

"I saw an urban fox with its cubs."

"It's" is only ever an abbreviation of "it is":

"It's up to you now!"

14. Lay/lie

"Lay" is a transitive verb which you do to something or someone else:

"The gardener must lay the turf for the new lawn today."

"Lie" is an intransitive verb, i.e. you can only do it to yourself:

"I really need to lie down now."

15. Less/fewer

"Less" refers to overall quantity, i.e. something big which shrinks:

"The amount of money in my savings account is less than it was last month."

"Fewer" should be used for individual units or numbers, so the sign above the quick checkout aisle in a supermarket should say:

"Six items or fewer."

16. Licence/license

"Licence" with a "c" is the noun (in UK English):

"Have you seen my driving licence anywhere?"

"License" with an "s" is the verb:

"James Bond 007 is licensed to kill."

17. Lose/loose

"Lose" is a verb:

"Have you managed to lose your wallet again?"

"Loose" is an adjective meaning the state of being unconstrained:

"Let the dogs loose!"

18. Practice/practise

"Practice" with a "c" is the noun:

"To become a good musician you need plenty of practice."

"Practise" with an "s" is the verb:

"He practises the violin every morning, which drives the neighbours insane."

19. Stationary/stationery

"Stationary" is an adjective meaning still or fixed:

"The car is stationary."

"Stationery" means letter paper, pens and so on.

20. e.g./i.e.

"e.g." means "for example":

"You will need to watch out for traps in the assault course, e.g. pot holes and trip wires."

"i.e." means "therefore" or "that is".

"I was caught out by the questions after my conference speech, i.e. I had failed to prepare myself adequately."

"i.e." can also be used before a statement that reiterates/clarifies the previous statement

"When writing advice letters, put your recommendation (i.e. what you would do in the client's shoes) in a prominent place."

21. Ampersand (&)

"&" is a shorthand symbol to represent "and"; it should only ever be used for names (e.g. Marks & Spencer, Ernst & Young etc.).

A little light relief...

Predictive text in mobile phones can often trip up the unwary, especially with longer words, so pay attention before you click "Send".

Some of the more embarrassing examples I have seen on the internet are: "Grandma just showed me her horse penis", when what the sender really meant was "horse pendant". Another reads: "You are the first girl I've ever thought about the führer with." That sender actually user meant: "thought about the future with". One mother received a text from her son to say he had made the university "cross-dressing team". He really intended to say the "cross-country" running team.

Chapter 5: Capital Letters and Numbering

Let us now consider some fairly well established conventions about capital letters, numbering and tabulation. If you follow these, your presentation will be truly professional.

Capital letters

There are essentially nine rules for using capital letters. If in doubt, modern style is to try to keep as many words in lower case as possible. Certainly some people see fit to apply capitals to the most bizarre words and phrases, as if they require some kind of extra dignity. I once read some blurb from an English vineyard extolling the delights of their wines and how one variety was "... especially important to our South East Restaurant Trade." You should use capital letters:

1. For the first letter of the first word in a sentence.
2. For personal names (e.g. John, Jake).
3. For days of the week (Sunday, Monday), months of the year (January, February) and public holidays (Christmas, Easter) but *not* seasons of the year (spring, summer, autumn, winter).
4. For official names of buildings, streets and other public places:

   "The Great Eastern Hotel is located on Liverpool Street."

5. For trade names.

   "Xerox photocopiers, Apple computers"

6. For the full names and all the abbreviated names of government agencies and departments:

   "Her Majesty's Revenue and Customs" / "HMRC"

7. For all official titles of honour and respect when they precede personal names:

   "Ms Mary Contrary", "Prime Minister David Cameron"

8. For all academic titles and religious titles when they precede a name:

   "Doctor Geoffrey Wong", "Professor Carol Feltham", "Bishop Evan Jones"

9. For academic degrees following a name, whether abbreviated or written out in full:

   "Patrick Farrell PhD", "John Trimbos MA (Oxon)"

10. For abbreviations if the words they stand for start with capital letters, such as professional qualifications:

    "Richard Mowbray FCCA, Carole Cornish FRICS"

11. For the first, last and all principal words of the titles of books, plays and television programmes:

    "A Tale of Two Cities", "News at Ten"

A little light relief...

Names are often fraught with difficulty when transferring from one language to another. Car manufacturers seem to be particularly unfortunate with models such as:

Rolls Royce Silver Mist (rapidly renamed when it translated into "Silver Crap" in German)

Chevrolet Nova (which translates into "No go" in Spanish)

Mitsubishi Pajero (at least it alliterates: Mitsubishi Masturbator in Spanish; obviously a tricky language)

Ford Pinto (apparently this is Brazilian Portuguese slang for "small penis")

Numbers

This is a fairly loose convention, in that it is easy to find exceptions, but the convention in business writing is to express numbers 1 to 10 as words (one, two, three etc.) and 11 and above as figures (11, 12, 13 etc.). But there are many cases where it would be odd not to write either a word or a figure, so here are the exceptional cases:

Express as words

1. Exact amounts when they begin a sentence:

   "Thirty companies are involved in the merger."

2. Smaller of two numbers when used together:

   "Two 8-file cabinets, 35 ten-file cabinets"

   ...just to avoid someone ordering 28 cabinets for your office by mistake.

3. Approximate amounts and fractions:

   "About a thousand attended the conference last week."

4. Ordinals in the middle of sentences:

   "The fourteenth employee to fall ill this year..."

5. Time, if the word "o'clock" is understood:

   "She left the office at eleven."

Express as figures

1. Dimensions and weights:

   "The room is 5 x 25 metres."

2. Dates in business:

   8 October 2017

3. Numbers following nouns such as page, chapter, room and rule:

   Rule 9, Page 16

A little light relief...

Here is a piece of American humour which I could not resist:

"The Assembly passed and sent to the Senate a bill requiring dog owners in New York City to clean up after their pets, in penalty of a $100 dollar fine. The bill also applies to Buffalo."

Structure, Presentation and Style

Chapter 6: Structuring and Presenting Your Writing

It is always a good discipline to set yourself an overall objective at the start of the writing process. Ask yourself what impact your work is supposed to have upon the reader; how is your work supposed to benefit the reader? What do you want to do – advise, educate, persuade, entertain, outline different options, a combination of these? Key to this is deciding on the best structure to guide the reader through your ideas and proposals. Managers often complain that documents are poorly and illogically structured, and indeed that they are often repetitious and convoluted. There are nine possible structures that work really well, and probably an almost infinite number of hybrids using elements of each. Here is the menu of structures:

Grouping ideas can break the text into more manageable chunks for the reader. For example, a document proposing a new product or service could be split into the following groups of ideas: production, fixed and variable costs, pricing strategy, target audience, marketing etc.

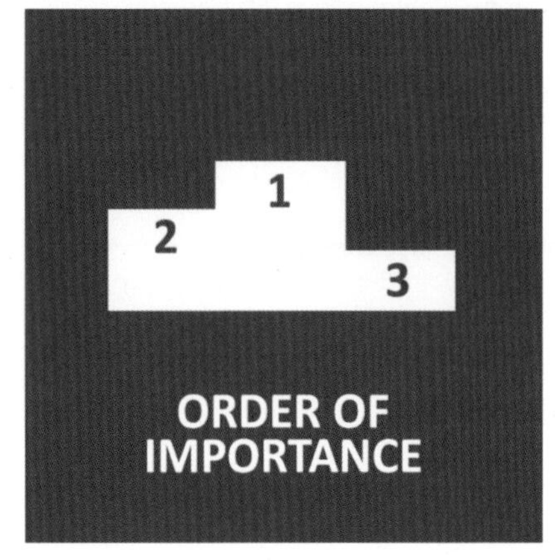

Ideas can be arranged from most to least important, or vice versa. For example, a quarterly report for managers might deal with the issues that are most pressing first in terms of urgency. This ranks information for the reader who has little time, and who needs to make a quick decision based on your feedback.

You could do this in four steps: (a) describe a problem; (b) give examples; (c) explain causes; (d) provide solutions. E.g. losing market share; facts and figures; inroads by new competitors; ideas for new product initiatives. This helps to explain crises/conflicts and manages the dissemination of bad news.

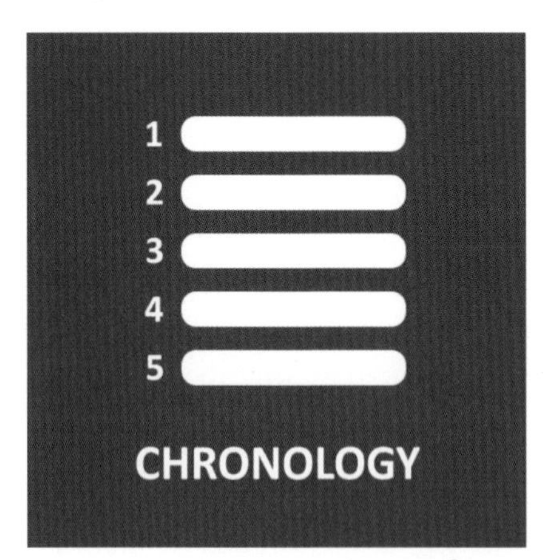

You can put things in time order, such as when describing new processes or projects. It helps to allay fears about whether a timetable is achievable. If, for example, you are outlining how you would run a potential project, then it probably makes sense for the reader to follow your ideas in sequence: (1) consultation (2) design (3) implementation (4) completion.

How – Who – What – Where – When – Why ("HW5"). This technique is great for narratives or descriptions of coming events: "John Jones, our new London training manager, will carry out a firm-wide training needs analysis in the coming month using this methodology, to help us enhance the training strategy."

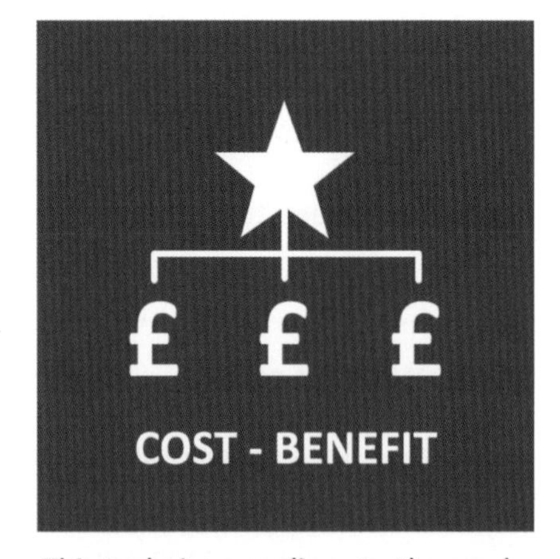

This technique outlines to the reader the potential benefits of an idea, followed by a breakdown of how much each element with cost. It works well for promoting new ideas, products or services. For example: "a new training programme could increase productivity by 50%. This would involve the following costs: venue hire, purchase of materials, tutor wages."

This builds on the reader's basic knowledge, and then educates them by progressing onto more complex ideas, e.g. describing the functions of an I.T. system, and then explaining how you can enhance it by dialling in new features and functions. It works well with a non-technical audience.

This works well for readers who need the big picture first, backed up by detail – or vice versa. E.g. the project must be delayed, because of: (a) design issues; (b) legal issues; (c) labour dispute; (d) budget overruns; (e) I.T. issues etc.

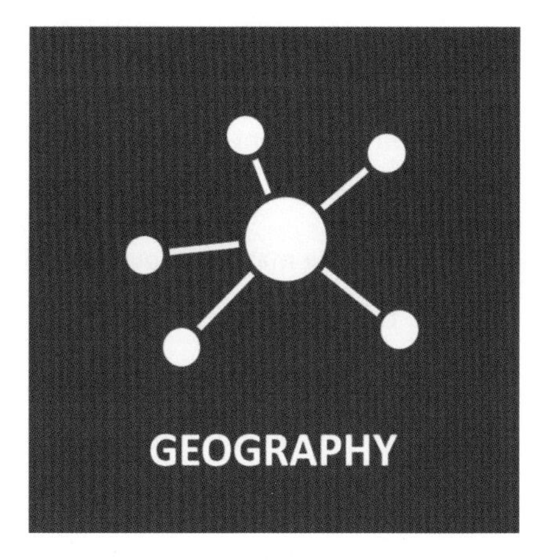

This might work for proposals covering an international network of offices, or, for example, a marketing strategy for target clients in different sectors or areas.

The important point here is that you should plan the structure in advance, rather than making it up as you go along. Making up the structure as you go along will give you a mushy structure, and the writing process will also take twice as long as it needs to. If necessary, write out a skeleton of your document first – just the headings and sub-headings – and juggle them around to give you the optimum structure. Sometimes there may be two or three structures that work for the same document, so just think about the reader's level of knowledge and state of mind and then choose the most effective option. You will also find that the word-for-word writing takes much less time if you have already written out the headings and given yourself a structure to follow.

A little light relief...

Use headings and paragraph breaks to move from one topic to another, so that the reader does not see a connection where none is intended. Here is another extract from a church newsletter:

"The low self-esteem help group will meet at 7pm on Tuesday. Please do not use the main entrance."

Presenting your work

The use of clear and accurate language obviously lies at the heart of effective business writing. Do not however overlook the need to present the page properly to make its layout reader-friendly. Here are the best practice rules for visual presentation:

- Widen margins; at least 3cm justified on the left and either justified or unjustified on the right. Double justification looks neater, but it creates uneven gaps between the words which can lead to increased eye strain in very long technical documents.
- Vary paragraph length to avoid huge blocks of text; the rule of thumb is that no paragraph should be more than about 15 lines long as it can be off-putting to the reader.
- Use headings and sub-headings to indicate a change of subject matter.
- Use tables, graphics, boxes and bullet points where appropriate.
- Choose the right font: Times New Roman is a common Serif font

Whereas Arial is an example of a Sans-Serif font

The general view in publishing is that Serif fonts (i.e. those with decorative embellishments) are easier on the reading eye, but that Sans-Serif fonts stand out well for headings and sub-headings. In any event never use more than two fonts in one document, or it will look too fussy.

Tabulation

Tabulation is brilliant for setting out a list of items in what would otherwise be an unfeasibly long sentence. Here is an example:

"The following matters should be taken into account when advising a company which is facing a hostile takeover:

(i) the relevant share price;

(ii) the strength of shareholder enthusiasm;

(iii) public opinion; and

(iv) the likely stance of the competition authorities."

Although not compulsory, it is usual to end each line with a semicolon; and the penultimate line should end with a semicolon and either the word "and" or the word "or". "And/or", although it withstands logical scrutiny, is dangerous because a lot of readers do not know whether you mean "and" or "or" or "at least one of these", so it is better to stick to "or" for non-exhaustive lists.

Here we therefore have the two great benefits of tabulation:

1. it makes it clear to the reader how many items are in the list; and
2. it emphasises that a list is either "conjunctive" (i.e. you must comply with all of the requirements) or "disjunctive" (i.e. you must comply with only one or more of these requirements").

There is a third reason for using tabulation, which is to avoid the ambiguities that can arise when using a long sentence with a list in it. Take for example: "You can qualify for benefits under the policy if you are 60 years or younger and incapacitated and the policy also provides benefits in the event that you are blinded in one eye or both eyes or are injured at work." What does this mean? It could mean:

"You can qualify for benefits if you are:

(i) under 60 and incapacitated;

(ii) blinded in one or both eyes; or

(iii) injured at work."

Or:

"You can qualify for benefits if you are 60 or under and:

(i) incapacitated;

(ii) blinded in one or both eyes; or

(iii) injured at work."

Or:

"You can qualify for benefits if you are:

(i) under 60 and incapacitated; or

(ii) blinded in one or both eyes or otherwise injured at work."

There are other slightly more bizarre permutations too. So my advice in this instance is pretty strict: if you have three or more items in a series, you must tabulate because to do otherwise is really quite dangerous.

A little light relief...

After all this talk of illness, blinding and so on I could not resist this medical typo:

"Mrs Johnson will be entering hospital this week for testes."

Chapter 7: Writing Style

Use your imagination

Use your imagination/creativity as well as logic when writing. It is always a good idea to set yourself an objective at the outset. Ask yourself: "What is my purpose in writing? How should my communication affect the reader?" Should it educate? Persuade? Amuse? Think about how you can use language to achieve your goal.

A lot of writing style guides and training courses emphasise plain English and grammar rules, and in doing so they make people think they should adopt a uniform approach to writing. While this is true to some extent, rules of style and grammar still leave more than enough room for individual creativity and originality.

This is especially important when writing persuasively, say in pitch documents to try to win new work. You could, for example, use words with a bit more emotional kick:

"This will damage/hurt/slash profitability"

...has more punch than:

"This will have a negative impact on profitability".

You could also use personal words to sound more human:

"If you have any questions please contact us"

...sounds much warmer than (but just as professional as):

"Any questions or enquiries should be addressed to this department".

Try to use words like "you/your" more than "I/me/we/us" because that will ensure you talk more to the reader than about yourself, which is probably one of the best ways to sound persuasive.

"We can provide unrivalled service for our clients"

....is less persuasive than:

"You will find that we can provide unrivalled service for your organisation".

Finally, do not be afraid to write something original or unusual. A nutritionist talking on the BBC once said this about obese children: "These children are digging their own graves with their knives and forks." This is brilliant imagery.

A little light relief...

Do not overdo it with your imagery, or indeed create unintended mental images. This is supposedly from a real letter sent to a local authority housing department:

"I want some repairs done to my cooker as it has backfired and burnt my knob off."

Be careful with jargon and clichés

Do think about whether the reader will understand any jargon or terms of art that you use regularly. It is also true that many jargon words have become hackneyed and overused, so when they appear in print they make the reader's mind switch off. Some examples that always make me groan are:

- "Paradigm shift" (meaning "major change")
- "Blue sky thinking" (meaning "generating new ideas")
- "Thinking outside the box" (meaning "thinking unconventionally")
- "Pushing the envelope" (meaning "being ambitious")
- "Wash its own face" (meaning "not make a loss")
- "Elephant in the room" (meaning "unmentioned problem")
- "Number crunching" (meaning "calculations")

The trouble with these is that they were clever once, but they have become so common that they suggest laziness in thinking by the writer.

Having said that, jargon and other expressions often convey powerful visual images and can therefore be quite persuasive at times. This is purely subjective so feel free to disagree, but the following do not make me groan and are still acceptable to me:

- As flat as a pancake
- Moving the goalposts
- Cool as a cucumber

Perhaps the answer lies in achieving some balance, maybe allowing yourself one piece of jargon per document or per chapter. Be open to new phrases as well before they turn into common jargon, for example "data rape" (i.e. stealing personal information from the internet); the use of the word "rape" is in itself shocking, but it certainly conveys the feelings of violation which victims of data theft often feel.

A little light relief...

Please do not write anything like this:

"This is an invitation to all my product evangelist colleagues. I think we need to touch base to have an ideas shower because, going forward, people have started to loop back to us about challenges they face when using our products. We need to look under the bonnet of our sales organisation to find ways to incentivise our colleagues to look beyond the low hanging fruit. I realise you can't turn an oil tanker around with a speed boat change, but these folks need to know that we've got them on our radar. So let's interface tomorrow, run some ideas up the flagpole and see who salutes. With any luck we'll all finish the day singing from the same hymn sheet."

The "KISS" principle

The acronym often used to describe the de-cluttering approach is **KISS**. There are two versions of this acronym: "**K**eep **I**t **S**hort and **S**imple" (the polite version) or "**K**eep it **S**imple, **S**tupid!" It depends on how rude you want to be when editing other people's work. The main point of this whole chapter is: if you have a simple idea, give it a nice, simple sentence.

Short sentences = clarity and impact

Be a CISSY: Clarity and Impact via Short Sentences – Yeah!

Getting carried away with the length of sentences is probably the worst sin that people commit in business writing. The consensus in writing style guides is that sentences should not really be more than 20 to 25 words long, but too many people ignore this in practice. I often run training sessions where delegates bring along examples of their recent written work, and I can guarantee that there will be at least one 55 word sentence waiting in the wings.

I once read about a readability study, which showed that a document with an average sentence length of 30 words has to be re-read in part by 95% of readers to extract its meaning. However, a document with an average sentence length of 20 words has to be re-read by only 5% of readers, so limiting sentence length is vital for readability. Another good rule of thumb is that a sentence should only have one main idea or concept, and in practice this seems to keep sentence length down.

I saw this recently in the office of a quango (quasi non-governmental organisation) in London:

"A signature on a delivery note or other documentation in connection with delivery of the Goods is evidence only of the number of packages received (and for the avoidance of doubt not evidence that the correct quantity of the actual Goods has been received or that the Goods are of appropriate quality or fit for purpose) and signature of such note or of any other acknowledgment will be deemed in all circumstances to be without prejudice to the Contracting Authority's rights including without limitation the right to reject the Goods and/or sue for damages for breach of this Contract by the Supplier."

This 103 word sentence is supposed to be intelligible to ordinary business people. It would be much better expressed in separate sentences and maybe even a bit of tabulation.

"A signature on a delivery note or other documentation relating to delivery of the Goods is evidence only of the number of packages received. It is not evidence that the correct quantity has been received as ordered, or that the Goods are of appropriate quality. A signature on behalf of the Contracting Authority will not affect its rights including:

- the right to reject the Goods; and
- the right to claim damages."

A little light relief…

You can go really bonkers with your sentence length if you like. Do not try to read this without drinking a stiff gin and tonic first, and certainly keep it away from children and those of a nervous disposition:

"In the event that the Purchaser defaults in the payment of any instalment of purchase price, taxes, insurance, interest, or the annual charge described elsewhere herein, or shall default in the performance of any other obligations set forth in this Contract, the Seller may: at his option: (a) Declare immediately due and payable the entire unpaid balance of purchase price and enforce conveyance of the land by termination of the contract or according to the terms hereof, in which case the Purchaser shall also be liable to the Seller for reasonable attorney's fees for services rendered by any attorney on behalf of the Seller, or (b) sell said land and premises or any part thereof at public auction, advertising in a newspaper of general circulation in the county or city in which the security property is located at least once a week for Three (3) successive weeks or for such period as applicable law may require and upon compliance by the Purchaser with the terms of sale, and upon judicial approval as may be required by law, convey said land and premises in fee simple to and at the cost of the Purchaser, and from the proceeds of the sale: FIRST to pay all proper costs and charges, including but not limited to court costs, advertising expenses, auctioneer's allowance, the expenses, if any required to correct any irregularity in the title, premium for Seller's bond, auditor's fee, attorney's fee, and all other expenses of sale occurred in and about the protection and execution of this contract, and all moneys advanced for taxes, assessments, insurance, and with interest thereon as provided herein, and all taxes due upon said land and premises at time of sale, and to retain as compensation a commission of five per cent (5%) on the amount of said sale or sales; SECOND, to pay the whole amount then remaining unpaid of the principal of said contract, and interest thereon to date of payment, whether the same shall be due or not, it being understood and agreed that upon such sale before maturity of the contract the balance thereof shall be immediately due and payable, THIRD, to pay liens of record against the security property according to their priority of lien and to the extent that funds remaining in the hands of the Seller are available; and LAST, to pay the remainder of said proceeds, if any, to the vendor.

Pay attention to word length too. I am not saying that long words are inherently bad, but one of the golden rules is never to use a long word where a short one will do. Many people seem to think that showing off their vocabulary makes them sound impressive, whereas in fact they really just sound stuffy and verbose. Also beware the same long word cropping up time and again in your writing – it will sound monotonous and make the reader switch off. My wife recently showed me a report which a colleague had emailed to her, containing the word "scenario" five times in one paragraph. I rest my case. Here is a list of long words, together with some one or two syllable alternatives:

Long Word	Short Word
Accommodate	House or meet
Acknowledge	Accept
Allocate	Share
Approximate	Rough
Assertive	Bold, strong or firm
Beneficial	Good or helpful
Collaboration	Venture or project
Consider	Review
Consolidate	Merge
Constitute	Make or is
Correlation	Trend or match
Demonstrate	Show
Deteriorate	Worsen or decline
Determine	Decide
Documented	Written
Enhancement	Upgrade
Establishment	Place
Examination	Test or research
Expenditure	Cost
Implementation	Start
Important	Vital
Incorporate	Include
Integration	Merger
Inevitable	Certain or sure

Long Word	Short Word
Information	Data or facts
Interface	Meet or contact
Investigate	Research
Negative	Bad
Operational	Work
Opportunities	Chances
Optimise	Enhance
Performance	Output
Pertinent	Apt
Possibility	Chance
Potential	Prospect
Principal	First, main or head
Prioritise	Rank
Productive	Useful
Quality	Standard or feature
Ramification	Result or upshot
Requirement	Need
Resolution	Outcome
Scenario	Case
Serendipitous	Lucky
Substantial	Large
Termination	End
Transitional	Ad hoc
Utilisation	Use

A little light relief...

Verbs are good, but please chose the right verb to convey your meaning. This is a letter written to a plumbing firm:

"Please send a man with clean tools to finish the job and satisfy the wife."

Base verbs

A good way to achieve the KISS principle is to use base verbs. Below is a list of common verbs, but for some reason a lot of people like to use two or three words instead of just one and they use a derivative form with a noun:

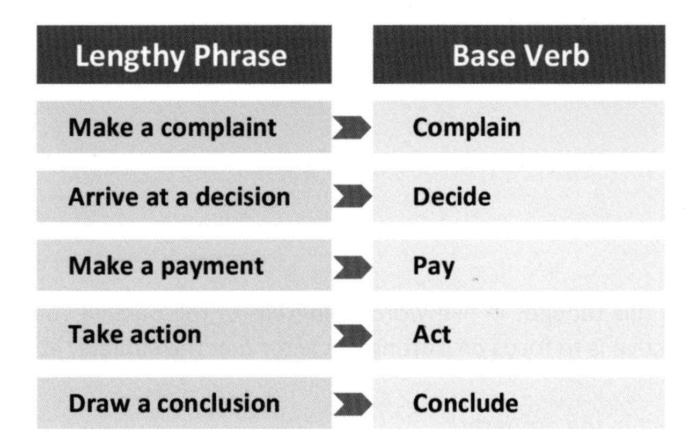

Lengthy Phrase	Base Verb
Make a complaint	Complain
Arrive at a decision	Decide
Make a payment	Pay
Take action	Act
Draw a conclusion	Conclude

Using the base verb is therefore a good way to cut out clutter, but professional writers say that verbs also provide much more emotional punch in writing. So if you want to make a really strong impression on the reader, use lots of verbs. The following sentence is supposed to have a strong impact (it is supposed to be borderline intimidating) but the derivative language has blunted all the impact:

"We are in sympathy with your point of view, but if it is your aim to cause a prolonging of our discussions, we will draw the conclusion that you do not want to enter into an agreement, and will take the necessary action to enter into negotiations with other interested parties."

What we really mean is:

"We understand your position, but if you drag out discussions we will decide that you do not want to agree terms, and we will negotiate with your main competitor."

Finally a lot of professions have their favourite word clusters, stock phrases which seem to crop up with monotonous regularity when one word will do the job really well. Here are some examples with some one or two word alternatives:

Word Cluster	Single Word	Word Cluster	Single Word
For the purpose of...	For	In respect of...	For or about
In accordance with...	Under	In some instances...	Sometimes
In close proximity to...	Near	It is within our power...	We can
In the event that...	If or when	Prior to...	Before
In light of...	Following	Subsequent to...	After
In relation to...	About	We are of the opinion that...	We believe or consider

A little light relief...

Be careful how you structure sentences as well. See this for example:

"Two estranged sisters were reunited after 18 years in a supermarket queue."

It often feels like I have been queuing for 18 years in the local supermarket, but this is ridiculous. If we structure sentences along the lines of "time-manner-place" then the meaning tends to become clearer:

"After 18 years two estranged sisters were reunited in a supermarket queue."

Active vs. passive voice

Using the active voice is one of the most basic, but most often broken, guidelines for writing clearly. Put simply, in the active voice *someone* does something:

> "*John* has written a book."

But in the passive voice something is done by someone to something or to someone else:

> "A book has been written by John."

In the active voice we can express this thought in five words, whereas in the passive voice we need seven. The best way to discipline yourself to write in the active is to focus on putting the actor (i.e. the subject) at the beginning of the sentence:

> "*The landlord* will rectify the defect in the property."

Not: "The defect in the property will be rectified by *the landlord*."

This whole principle becomes more serious for longer sentences and paragraphs, like this piece of passive voice rubbish:

> "The judge then turned to the application which had been made by the claimant for an injunction. In response to that request, the submission was made by the defendant that this form of discretionary relief was not appropriate because of the fact that the relevant clause was already null and void by reason of the prior order of the court. Therefore the said clause could have no further application and the defendant argued that in such circumstances full relief could be given without the grant of the injunction. The court found itself to be in agreement with that submission."

In the active voice, and with a bit of judicious pruning, we can more than cut the word count in half:

> "The judge then turned to the claimant's application for an injunction. The defendant submitted that a previous court order had rendered the relevant clause void, and that the court could give full relief without an injunction. The judge agreed with this argument."

The passive voice can also be dangerously vague about who does what:

> "It is felt that insufficient steps are being taken to boost our marketing drive."

Who feels this way? And who is supposed to be boosting the marketing drive? The passive voice often fails to answer these questions, whereas the active voice compels you to deal with them:

> "The board feels that the advertising department is failing..."

Of course it is possible that the writer or speaker here has used the passive voice deliberately to be a little vague, in the interests of diplomacy. You could also use this technique yourself if you want to avoid the glare of blame being turned on you. It is strongly rumoured that a former UK prime minister, when talking about his government's failure to regulate the banking sector, said in a speech, "Mistakes have been made..."

He probably did not want to be terribly specific here, perhaps by saying, "I made some mistakes..." or "My government has made mistakes."

There are other cases where the passive does seem to work better than the active voice, so it is good to remember that writing style pointers are guidelines rather than absolute rules. You can therefore legitimately use the passive in these examples:

When the actor is unknown or indefinite:

> "The shop was burgled"

(rather than: "A burglar has burgled the shop").

When the action is more important than the actor:

"The Annual General Meeting of the company has been called for next month."

Where you talk in general terms about whole populations, species or classes of people (the so-called "detached abstraction"):

"All children are created with a thirst for knowledge."

A little light relief...

Headline seen in a local newspaper: "Enraged cow injures farmer with axe."

This is another example of where the passive voice would actually have worked better: "Axe wielding farmer injured by enraged cow".

Simple sentences are usually more effective:

I found the following in a staff handbook:

"Should the supply of Post-it notes not be sufficient to meet your requirements, an application should be made to this department for a supply of additional packets."

Instead of using 27 words, maybe 7 would do:

"If you need Post-its call extension 1234."

A little light relief...

This is terribly unfair, but I am going to reprint it anyway. It comes from the packet instructions on a Japanese haemorrhoid relief product and it obviously lost a certain something in translation:

"Lie down on bed and insert Poscool slowly up to the projected portion like a sword-guard into anal duct. While inserting Poscool for approximately five minutes, keep quiet."

I will leave it up to you to make up your own KISS alternative.

Proof Reading and Editing

These terms ("proof reading" and "editing") are often used interchangeably, but do regard them as separate processes. Proof reading involves ironing out mistakes and inconsistencies, whereas editing focuses on improving style and making the document as reader-friendly as possible.

Often, documents like tenders (offers to supply goods or services) will include contributions from different people in different departments. The initial drafts may look disjointed if those contributors have different writing styles, which is likely to be the case. It is therefore good practice to edit the style to ensure the whole document provides a more cohesive and professional reading experience.

Chapter 8: Readability Statistics

It is a little known fact that you can set Microsoft Word to display an objective readability score for your documents. Readability in this context means that the information is clear to the reader and that he or she will have no problem understanding the language. Although any computer program is fallible, readability scores based on mathematical formulae do provide some critical objectivity, although your primary tool must of course remain your brain.

There are two tests: the Flesch Reading Ease and the Flesch–Kincaid Grade Level. They use the same core measures (word length and sentence length) and were both devised by the writer Rudolf Flesch.

The Flesch–Kincaid (F–K) reading grade level was developed under contract to the United States Navy in 1975 by J. Peter Kincaid, and it indicates the school grade level you need to be at in order to understand a piece of writing without any difficulty. It was first used by the US Army for assessing the difficulty of technical manuals in 1978 and soon after became the Department of Defense military standard. The Commonwealth of Pennsylvania was the first state in the US to require that automobile insurance policies be written at no higher than a ninth grade level of reading difficulty formula. This is now a common requirement in many other states and for other legal documents such as insurance policies.

In the Flesch Reading Ease test, higher scores indicate material that is easier to read; lower numbers mark passages that are more difficult to read. The formula for the Flesch Reading Ease Score (FRES) test is:

Readability Score	Audience
90.0–100.0	Easily understood by an average 11-year-old student
60.0–70.0	Easily understood by 13- to 15-year-old students
0.0–30.0	Best understood by university graduates

Reader's Digest magazine has a readability index of about 65; Time magazine scores about 52; an average 11-year-old student's written assignment has a readability test of 60–70, and the Harvard Law Review has a general readability score in the low 30s.

These readability tests are used extensively in the field of education. The "Flesch–Kincaid Grade Level Formula" translates the 0–100 score to a US grade level, making it easier for teachers, parents and librarians to judge the readability level of various books.

You can access these tools in Microsoft Word by clicking through the following options:

Microsoft Word (PC): File > Proofing > Options > then tick the "Show readability statistics" box

Microsoft Word (Mac): Word > Preferences > Spelling and Grammar > then tick the "Show readability statistics" box.

When you have finished using the Spelling and Grammar check, a box will appear on screen with several statistics, most of which (like word and character count) are of limited interest to us. There will however be the following:

- average words per sentence – this should be less than 20 overall;
- the percentage of passive sentences – which should be as close to zero as possible;
- Flesch Reading Ease – which should be as high as possible;
- Flesch-Kincaid Grade Level – e.g. a grade level of 12 equates to a sixth former; a grade level of 8 equates to a 12 to 13 year old.

To the right is a set of readability statistics for one of the chapters in this book. My esteemed editor originally presented me with statistics for the whole book and told me that my writing style was therefore horrendous – until I pointed out that the book contains examples of how not to write. So this is much more representative of how I write and my reputation as a paragon of clarity is now restored (thank goodness).

Readability Statistics	
Counts	
Words	1312
Characters	6224
Paragraphs	95
Sentences	68
Averages	
Sentences per Paragraph	1.6
Words per Sentence	13.8
Characters per Word	4.5
Readability	
Passive Sentences	1%
Flesch Reading Ease	70.1
Flesch-Kincaid Grade Level	6.9
	OK

A little light relief...

It is possible to push simplicity too far, for example (seen on a box for a shower cap provided by a hotel):

"Fits one head."

Chapter 9: Proof Reading Tips and Methods

Proof reading tips

Proof reading can often be tedious and time consuming, so here are some useful guidelines to save time and enhance accuracy. Distance yourself from any document you have just composed or typed. It is easy to miss mistakes in work you have produced. Whenever possible, put time between the composing and the proof reading. When you return to correct your work, you will be more objective and vigilant. Plan to proof read every piece of work at least once, to catch the errors and avoid costly corrections. This includes emails and informal internal business correspondence!

Get someone else to do it
(Not as facetious as it sounds)

Make it strange to yourself
Distance yourself from the content – go away and make some tea or preferably leave it overnight and then look again with fresh eyes

Read it aloud
Read slowly and concentrate

Check the headings

Check the overall numbering system for inconsistencies
Are you using (1) or 1., (a) or a. throughout?

Detect missing/duplicated items
Read aloud when checking numbers in sequence, digit by digit

Avoid line skipping
Place a straight edge (ruler, piece of paper) below the line you are reading to avoid skipping words or lines of text

Double-space text in draft form
This makes for easy proof-reading

Check references for accuracy
E.g. check that the table of contents/glossary correlate with the actual location of sections/words in the document

Make your formatting consistent
E.g. check your headings, font(s), line spacing, bullet points etc. are consistent

Take care when copying and pasting
When copying and pasting from one document to another or from a document to an email, often the fonts or formatting will be inconsistent and need to be tidied up to look suitably professional. There is also a very real risk that you will accidentally paste information that you did not intend future recipients of the document to read

A little light relief...

I once copied some text from an email and inadvertently left in the words "XXXXX might be talking complete rubbish but we ought to look into this." Unfortunately Mr XXXXX was one of the readers of the document (although to be fair he did talk monumental amounts of rubbish).

Proof reading methods

There are several methods of proof reading which some people find more useful than others.

Comparison method

Place the original version close to the updated or corrected copy. Move your eyes back and forth between the two. Hold a ruler or a pen/pencil (or if nothing else your fingers) on the original and corrected copy and follow along as you read. Sometimes it is possible to set the original on top of the corrected copy and hold both up to the light. Any discrepancies can be seen by using this technique. Be careful not to lose your place. Avoid distractions as much as possible. Errors occur when you take your eyes and your attention off your text.

Proof reading with a partner

Reading with a partner is a good way to check work. One partner checks the final copy while the other reads aloud. The writer/transcriber should always read out loud whilst the partner checks, since it is easier to spot the mistakes made by someone else. Though time-consuming, the partner method is recommended when checking important material, long columns of numbers and final drafts.

Proof reading alone

Read the work out loud: when you read aloud (or move your lips and form each word) you are forced to slow down and examine each word. You listen more attentively than you read and therefore notice mistakes more readily. To force yourself to look at individual words, try reading material from right to left or from the bottom of the page to the top. Reading backward helps when you are checking details such as spelling, but it is not effective for checking the accuracy of the content.

Proof reading from a computer screen

Enlarge the type - errors are more likely to stand out in a larger type font. Slowly scroll your document down line by line on the first reading, or use a straight edge against the screen to prevent your eyes from darting. Keep your screen and hard copy at the same place in the document - corrections and updates will be easier and faster, and hold the original next to the computer screen and use the comparison method of proof-reading.

A little light relief...

This is a letter which I produced to try to fool the Microsoft Word Spelling and Grammar checker. It looks immaculate on the computer screen (no red or green underlining) but it is actually riddled with typos. When I emailed it to every lawyer and training manager I know, nobody spotted everything. The only person who achieved 100% accuracy was a professional translator, but I suppose he has to be eagle-eyed in his profession. Here is the letter – see how well you do (the answers are on the next page).

Dear Mr...

Thank you for your inquiry about out contract drafting capabilities. We are continuously contacted by clients for such services, and we always insure that they are treated to the highest levels of service.

We are always very careful to advice you of all the necessary legal implications. You should also be aware that there are discreet processes to follow in the various jurisdictions you have mentioned. Any overseas lawyers instructed by us will have the relevant license to practice in that country.

The law is never stationery; it is always developing and changing. The agreement between the panties must be robust to stand the test of time. We are always vigilant for changes in the law – we never become disinterested.

Yours faithfully...

Solution

Dear Mr…

Thank you for your **enquiry** about **our** contract drafting capabilities. We are **continually** contacted by clients for such services, and we always **ensure** that they are treated to the highest levels of service.

We are always very careful to **advise** you of all the necessary legal implications. You should also be aware that there are **discrete** processes to follow in the various jurisdictions you have mentioned. Any overseas lawyers instructed by us will have the relevant **licence** to **practise** in that country.

The law is never **stationary**; it is always developing and changing. The agreement between the **parties** must be robust to stand the test of time. We are always vigilant for changes in the law – we never become **uninterested**.

Yours **sincerely**…

Note 1: this is written in UK English.

Note 2: "the agreement between the panties" was a real typo many years ago when I was training to be a solicitor, and my firm had a secretary whose heart was not in the job. She was actually typing a letter about a divorce case involving lots of steamy adultery, so her thoughts were probably on those details rather than on legal technicalities. I also once had a lawyer on a course in Bristol who thought it should have read: "the agreement between the pasties" – clearly he was thinking hard about his lunch.

Either way, you cannot trust spell checker if the typo is still a correct word – so be vigilant. It is also rumoured that the same secretary typed "shift work" in a witness statement without the "f", but this may be apocryphal.

Business Documents, Correspondence and Presentations

Although you regularly see articles in the press about the decline of the art of writing, it has ironically never been a more important business skill. We do so much work online these days and of course emails and websites rely largely on the written word. This chapter will therefore focus on best practice for all types of business writing: emails, letters, reports, articles, PowerPoint and minutes. I have also set out some examples of good and bad practice for you to refer to for inspiration, but bear in mind that there will often be several ways to express an idea.

Chapter 10: House Style

Many organisations have a house style for documents, which is of particular importance for lengthy things like reports and contracts. It is important to follow house style to maintain the professionalism and consistency of the company's output. This can help to strengthen the company's brand to clients.

House style guides vary a lot, with some going into much more detail than others. For example, some give guidance on the rules of plain English and preferred spellings, whereas others do not and simply focus on presentation points. Most, however, deal with the following issues. For larger companies at least, there tends to be a bank of templates available on the company's intranet, for letters, memos, Microsoft PowerPoint presentations, contracts, board minutes etc.

- **Fonts:** most organisations choose just one preferred font whereas others may have one for headings/titles and another for paragraphs of text.
- **Headings:** size, colour and font.
- **Bullet points**: square, round or something else like arrows.
- **Tables:** colour, format (e.g. whether to show the edges with lines or to leave them invisible.)
- **Page layout:** single or double justification.
- **Brand:** preferred use of company names and trademarks.
- **Dates and times**: most organisations set out dates like this: 3 January 2017; rather than 3rd January 2017. They may also specify how to express time: 5.30pm, 5:30pm, 17.30, 17:30, 17.30hrs, 17:30hrs.
- **Presentation of names and addresses**: most organisations do not use punctuation and prefer to set out address like this:

Mr R Jones
120 Heath Street
Hampstead
London
NW3 1DR

Similarly it is now common not to put commas after salutations and valedictions:

A little light relief...

The following are supposedly taken from insurance claim reports:

- The accident was due to the road bending.
- To avoid collision I ran into the other car.
- I collided with a stationary tree.
- I bumped into a shop window and sustained injuries to my wife.
- I misjudged a lady crossing the road.
- Coming home I drove into the wrong house and collided with a tree I haven't got.
- A pedestrian hit and went underneath my car.
- The car in front stopped suddenly and I crashed gently into him.
- The other car bumped into me without warning me of his intention.
- I unfortunately ran over a pedestrian and the old gentleman was taken into hospital, much regretting the circumstances.
- I consider neither vehicle was to blame, but if either was it was the other one.
- I knocked over a man, he admitted it was his fault as he had been knocked down before.

Chapter 11: Business Emails

It is only in recent years that people have begun to realise that there is a real art to writing effective emails. The main problems with emails are that:

- they create enormous pressure on the receiver to respond quickly;
- most people receive too many emails, so they are disinclined to read them properly;
- many people now habitually read emails on their mobile phones, so the main message has to be front-loaded to grab their attention;
- once an ill thought out or inappropriate email leaks out into the public domain, then it is like Pandora's box – it can never be shut away again.

Having said that, emails are of course wonderful for communicating quickly to many recipients, across time zones and to send attachments. I wonder how we ever managed without them. After much agonising I have now worked out ten commandments for writing an effective email. You need to follow these visually in your mind's eye as if you were staring at the top of your computer screen and working your way downwards.

1. **Choose the right recipients**

   There are two elements to this: (1) do not overload unnecessary recipients with your email, but do not leave anyone out either; and (2) check your addresses carefully since Microsoft Outlook and similar programs often try to guess email addresses once you start typing. For example, if I type "lu" into my own laptop two addressees called Lucy appear – one is a training manager at a law firm and the other is my wife; I can think of all kinds of confusion if I picked the wrong Lucy by mistake.

2. **Write an intelligent subject heading**

   If you write too much then the text will disappear in a trail of full stops... But you can also put in too little. A few years ago I did some work with a real estate lawyer who had worked on the redevelopment of The Oval cricket ground in London, and she said that she had received over four hundred emails all saying "The Oval" in the subject heading. This is practically useless (so are headings like "Meeting", "update", "Next Week" and so on). Try to give the name of the project and just a little extra about which aspect you are talking about, such as: "The Oval – Disposal of surplus land" or "The Oval – Agenda for next team meeting".

3. **Insert any attachments**

   I always used to do this at the end, but I often forgot and had to send follow-on emails saying something like, "Oops! Forgot the attachment." Not very professional. Since I started adding the attachments up front, I have never had to send an "Oops!" email again.

4. **Decide on the right form of salutation**

   There seems to be a consensus these days on how to sign off – "Yours sincerely" and "Yours faithfully" are reckoned to be too formal, so use "Regards" or "Kind regards" instead. But the opening salutation is a minefield. I get emails from many different organisations and the openings are all over the place. The most formal start with "Dear John"; slightly less formal is to state the name only – "John"; and a surprising number start very informally – "Hi John – how are you today?" If you know the recipient well then you can decide on the level of formality needed, but if in doubt err on the side of formality. You can always relax your writing style if the response is chatty and informal, but moving the other way is more awkward.

5. **Write a really strong opening**

   In other words, tell the reader why they need to read your email: "Here are the notes from this morning's project meeting", "We now have the result of the arbitration hearing" and so on. You can put details in the following paragraphs, but always make the really important point in the first sentence. A training manager recently told me of a firm-wide email from his I.T. department about a significant computer upgrade, but the relevance to individual staff members was buried away halfway down the first page. I wonder how many employees bothered to read that far.

6. **Edit the language after typing your main text**

   Try to de-clutter as much as possible to make the language clear and direct.

7. **Aids to readability**

   Add in (for example) headings or bullet points if they help to de-construct the information and make it more user-friendly.

8. **Spell check**

   Run spell checker through the email. Proof reading for typos is always more difficult on a computer screen than on a hard copy, so use the built-in aids to check for accuracy and to avoid howlers.

9. **Say what you need from the recipient**

   Say what you want from the reader before you sign off: "I look forward to receiving your instructions before the close of business tomorrow"; "Please read the attached notes carefully before the court hearing next week".

10. **Email signature**

    Attach your email signature with all your contact details in case the reader needs to get hold of you urgently. A signature should at the very least include your name, position, company, contact number and email address. Consider also including your daytime number (if different from your mobile number), fax number (if relevant), business address and business website address. Here is a typical email signature:

Rachel Aquinas
Training Coordinator

Greensleeves Global Services Manila Inc.
8th Floor Corporate Center, #3030 11th Avenue, Taguig City, Philippines 1635
Tel: +44 (0)20 7859 1122 I Fax: +44 (0)20 7859 3344
Email: rachel.aquinas@greensleeves.com

A little light relief...

For some reason humour and irony do not seem to translate well into the email format, so the general advice is to refrain and to save these for the follow-up telephone call. However, emails can sometimes give rise to unintentional humour, and the following true life story also illustrates how you have to be careful with technology like spell checker too.

This was told to me by the training partner in a transatlantic law firm. One of their trainees had to compose a long email to a client with a slightly unusual surname, "Mr Braithwaites". I have an unusual surname myself which originates in Holland, so I sympathise because spell checker always tries to turn my name into "John Thrombosis". Anyway, the nervous trainee ran spell checker through the email, forgot to notice the name, clicked on "send" – and sent off an email starting "Dear Mr Buttocks". You cannot make this stuff up...

Examples of bad emails

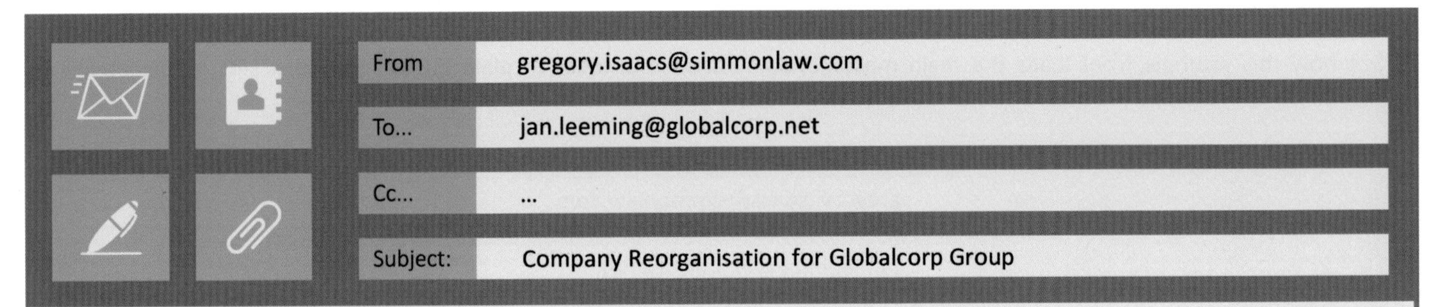

Dear Jan

Company Reorganisation for Globalcorp Group

I write further to our telephonic interface in order to advise you concerning the legal framework for the company and its subsidiaries together with a possible organisational structure that you may consider appropriate in all of the circumstances. I know you need to convey this advice to key members of the board and have therefore drafted this advice as concisely as possible. I should make it clear from the outset that, in normal circumstances, and notwithstanding any other relevant considerations or arrangements, a Group health and safety strategy should protect the parent company and its directors from any corporate and indeed personal liability. In those circumstances the Group plc should absolutely not seek to interfere in the normal day to day running operations of the subsidiary companies as this could very well make the parent company and its board liable within the existing framework of the law and therefore subject to criminal responsibilities as well as civil claims. I am nevertheless conscious that for some group structures there is frequently felt a need by the parent plc to effect a health and safety strategy which is seen to work not only on paper but also in practice.

With the above in mind the suggested organisational structure which is perhaps more easily justifiable is one which endeavours to protect the board of directors of the Group plc or Group holding company from any personal liability should an unfortunate episode take place. The alternative would be the scenario where a director of the board has been identified as responsible for ensuring that the health and safety policy is put into practice. If that is the case then an alternative structure should be put into place but with the proviso that should there be a serious occurrence then it will be that director who will be looked upon as being, in legal terminology, the embodiment of the board and therefore it will be the actions of this director which the Health and Safety Executive would be bound to investigate. The first alternative would involve the creation of a corporate safety steering committee whilst the second alternative puts the onus on the board of directors or alternatively a named director to oversee health and safety. On balance, and taking into consideration the preliminary research carried out by the writer's esteemed assistant, one tends to prefer the option in which the terms of the corporate safety steering committee would be one where the overall strategy is promulgated by the parent company but the operational ramifications would lie with each individual subsidiary company who would be responsible for ensuring the day to day health and safety of its staff. The use of the corporate safety steering committee is a not uncommon practice.

I trust this makes everything clear. I remain available to answer any requests for clarification or elucidation as you may have.

Yours sincerely

Gregory Isaacs

The above example is too long - impenetrable and verbose. There is no need to actually read the whole thing. The example below goes too far the other way however. You can be too broad-brush in writing advice, and the tone, exclamation marks and emoticon are clearly inappropriate for business correspondence. [LOL!]

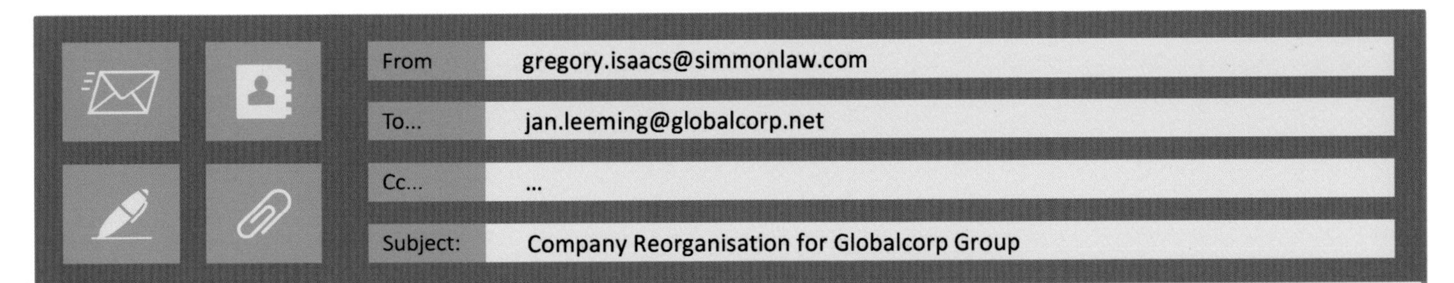

Hi Jan!

Company Reorganisation for Globalcorp Group

Sorry for the delay in coming back to you – I got absolutely bladdered over the weekend! The answer's simple really – set up a set of Corporate Safety Steering Committees to take all the hassle. Easy!

LOL

Greggers xxx

Example of a good email – the right balance

See how this example front loads the main message, summarises the ideas in plain English and uses aids to readability (headings) to break up the information to make it more readable.

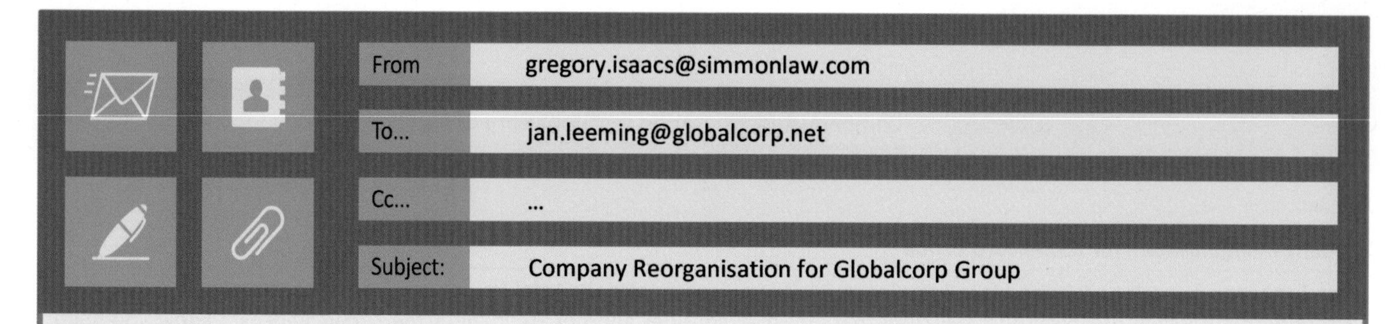

Dear Jan

Thank you for your telephone call earlier today. As promised I have done some initial research into the best way to deal with health and safety strategy with the Group, and it seems to me that there are two real options to consider.

Option 1 – corporate safety steering committees

Under this option each company subsidiary would set up its own committee to deal with health and safety strategy and policies. The main advantage of this is that the Group holding company cannot be held liable if there is a breach of health and safety legislation. The potential downside is that it can become difficult to establish and maintain common standards and policies across the Group subsidiaries, and I appreciate how important this is to you and your colleagues.

Option 2 – nominated Group director to oversee health and safety strategy

The alternative would be to reserve the making of health and safety policy to the Group holding company with a nominated director on the main board in charge. This is the better option for establishing common standards and policies across all of the subsidiary companies, but on the other hand this potentially attached liability to the holding company and even to that director, in both civil and criminal law.

Preliminary advice

Following our conversation my assistant has done some research across the FTSE Top 100, and it seems that allowing each company its own corporate safety steering committee is by far the more popular option. Given the overall management structure across the Group I am sure that you would have no difficulty in ensuring common standards across the Group. On balance this is therefore my initial recommendation to you.

Kind regards

Gregory Isaacs

Legal Counsel

Excellence LLP

www.citycareerseries.com
@career_series
+44 (0)77 670 21811
information@citycareerseries.com

Chapter 12: Formal Letters

The emerging rule of thumb is that an email should only be an A4 page long when printed out, so if a business communication is likely to be longer then it should really be written as a proper letter. By all means send it out by email, but if it comes out as a Microsoft Word attachment the reader is likely to pay it proper attention.

Just like any other form of business writing, business letters are written for a purpose. It is worthwhile knowing what that purpose is then, so every aspect of the letter is geared to achieving it.

There will be times when you feel the need to dash off a vitriolic letter full of anger, criticism and threats. If your intention is simply to let off steam, like writing a letter to The Times, then by all means do so; but if your intention is to persuade someone to do something, such as pay an outstanding bill, it may be wise to think again.

Structure

1. Start by writing to a person by name

If you do not know who to write to, ring up and ask. Be sure to find out:

- how to spell their name;
- their position in the company; and
- how they prefer to be addressed, e.g. Mrs, Miss, or Ms

2. The heading

Use a heading that identifies precisely and concisely what the letter is about. Emboldening is usual to make this stand out (see the below example). These days, there is no need to start the letter with "Re".

3. Opening

The opening of the letter should establish:

- a link with the last contact you had with the recipient, e.g. reference to a previous letter or phone call; and
- why you are writing.

There is no need to repeat the heading in the opening of the letter or to refer to it in the first sentence in any other way. Thank you is always a good opener. It is polite, friendly and helps to get them on your side, and often there will genuinely be something to thank them for - their letter, their phone call, their time, etc.

If an apology is appropriate, the opening is a good place for it. Remember, you can say sorry without admitting liability. You could say: "I was sorry to hear you were not happy with the service you received." It makes no actual comment about the service; it simply says that you are sorry that your client is unhappy.

4. The detail

The middle of the letter sets out the detail. Keep to the point, giving only the necessary detail. If the letter goes beyond one page, your reader will have to be very interested to read it all.

5. Close

The close of the letter tells the reader what happens next. What should they do? What will you do? Leave the reader in no doubt. If you are writing a sales letter, try to retain the initiative. Rather than asking them to contact you, tell them that you will call them in a few days' time. If the letter is lengthy, a quick summary of the key points may be helpful.

Starting and finishing letters

The better you know the person you are writing to, the more flexibility you have in how you greet them and bid them farewell. "Hi!" is fine when writing to friends, but this is rarely acceptable in formal business correspondence, particularly if the letter is to be kept on file. For the more formal type of business letter there are rules to guide us.

Dear Sirs...

This form is used when writing to an organisation in general, rather than a specific person within it.

Dear Sir (or Dear Madam)...

This style is used less and less in modern business correspondence, although some traditional organisations have yet to let it go. It is appropriate when the addressee is known to be male or female, but tradition or circumstances dictate extreme formality.

Dear Sir or Madam...

Again, this is becoming very rare. It suggests that the letter is to a specific individual, but the writer has not taken the trouble to find out their name, or even whether they are male or female. Unless you have to use one of the earlier forms, it will usually be best to get to know the addressee's name and then use it.

Dear Mr Jones...

Names and titles are very personal and if you are going to use them they must be correct.

Remember, the purpose of writing a letter will often be to get the reader to do something; so do not make the task more difficult by getting off on the wrong foot. Do not assume that every man is addressed as "Mr" - he might be a "Dr", "Professor" or "Lord". For a woman, there are more options. Is she "Mrs", "Miss", "Ms" or is she a "Dr" or "Lady"? Guessing is too risky. If in doubt, ask. Ring up and ask a secretary or receptionist how the person prefers to be addressed, how they spell their name and their precise job title. If you are meeting the person then ask for a business card for future reference.

Dear Chris...

Use first names with care and only when you feel you know them well enough.

Consider the below when deciding whether or not to use first names:

- Have you spoken to them on the phone? Have you met them? How long have you known them?
- How did they introduce themselves? How do they address you?
- How do they sign their letters - initials and surname, first and surname, first name only?
- What is their position in relation to yours - senior, junior, supplier, agent, client?
- What is the norm in that company or industry?

Never modify their name unless they invite you to. If someone introduces himself as Christopher, do not change it to Chris.

The formal close of the letter will depend on the opening. Here are some examples:

Opening	Close
Dear Sir/Madam	Yours faithfully
Dear Mr/Mrs/Miss/Ms Smith	Yours sincerely
	Yours truly *(this is a less formal option)*
Dear Chris	Yours sincerely
	Yours
	Yours truly
	Best wishes
	Kind regards

One way to remember whether to use "sincerely" or something else at the end of the letter is to think: never have "s" at both the opening and the close of a letter (i.e. "S"ir and "S"incerely). If you start with "Sir" (or "Madam"), then end with "Yours faithfully". If you do not (e.g. you start with "Mr"/"Mrs" or the person's name), then use "Yours sincerely" or one of the other options listed to the left.

Sometimes people handwrite the salutation and the sign-off. This adds a personal touch, which can be very effective if you know the person or have at least spoken to them. It should not be used if you are sending a standard letter because it will then display laziness and a lack of respect for your reader as an individual (i.e. it will look like you could not even be bothered to edit the standard letter on the computer).

Cutting the clichés

There are many expressions that have been used so frequently in letters that they have come to have no meaning, or in some cases they just sound silly. They are usually wordy and imprecise expressions that at best make the writer sound pompous and unfriendly, and at worst obscure the message in the letter. Here are some expressions to avoid ("commercialese") and some suggested alternatives ("plain English"), although in some cases it is better to say nothing:

Openers to avoid	Better options
Further to your letter of...	Thank you for your letter of...
Further to the above matter...	(Unnecessary – just leave it out)
With reference to your letter of...	I was pleased to receive your letter of...
We note what you say	(Avoid – this tends to suggest disagreement)
Your comments have been noted	(Ditto – avoid)
We are in receipt of...	We have received...
We acknowledge receipt of...	We have received...
It has come to my attention that...	I see that...
It has been brought to my attention...	I note that...
We are obliged to you for...	Thank you for...

Middles to avoid	Better options
You claim or state that you sent...	We cannot trace your...
We should respectfully remind you...	Please remember that...
We regret to inform you...	Unfortunately...
Your problem...	The problem... (sounds less accusing)
In very short order	Quickly or soon...
At your earliest convenience	As soon as possible...

Closures to avoid	Better options
I trust this information meets your...	I hope I have been able to answer...
Assuring you of our best attention	(Avoid)
Please do not hesitate to contact me	Please call me
Looking forward to your response	I look forward to your reply
Enclosed please find...	I enclose...
I remain your obedient servant	(Just no! Never)
Thanking you in anticipation of...	Many thanks

Replying to complaint letters

There are three main types of complaints and they can best be dealt with by following the simple guidelines given below:

1. We are wrong and must admit it

- Thank you for your letter
- I am sorry
- Explain what happened
- Say what will be done
- Yours sincerely

2. We are right but in the interests of public relations will meet the claim

- Thank you for your letter
- Sympathise - show concern
- Say what we are prepared to do
- Explain how to prevent the same thing happening again
- Yours sincerely

3. We are right and not prepared to meet the claim

- Thank you for your letter
- Sympathise
- I can understand your point
- However, this is our point
- Because of our point we can't help
- Explain how to prevent similar occurrence in future
- Yours sincerely

A little light relief...

From a company complaints brochure: "If you think our products are unsatisfactory, you should see our manager."

Example of a bad letter

Metropolitan Bank plc

Dead Mrs O'Connor

Re: Your dead husband

I refer to the abovementioned matter. I am sorry to have troubled you by sending your husband our latest private banking brochure so soon after his death, especially as it contains details of so many exciting and innovative financial services. If there is anything you wish to discuss from the brochure please do not hesitate to contact me.

Meanwhile I hope you continue to enjoy the benefits of our high interest current account.

Assuring you of our best attention at all times.

Yours faithfully

Jean McDonald

Apart from the crass tone and commercialese, you win bonus points by spotting the typo ("Dead Mrs O'Connor") and the incorrect layout and sign-off. Below is a better letter.

Example of a good letter

Metropolitan Bank plc

Customer Services

Gutter Lane

London EC1 4FU

17 January 2017

Mrs M O'Connor

27 Waldron Avenue

London

SE11 5PO

Dear Mrs O'Connor

Your late husband

I am sorry to have troubled you by sending your husband our latest private banking brochure so soon after his death. Please accept my sincerest apologies.

I have amended our records and assure you that this will not happen again.

If I can be of any assistance with your banking affairs please contact me.

Yours sincerely

Jean McDonald

Customer Care Adviser

This letter is diplomatic, polite, succinct and says what the writer will do to rectify the problem. Sometimes things go wrong and it is necessary to say sorry.

Chapter 13: Reports

Winston Churchill's circular

This is what the Prime Minister wrote to all Government Departments in August 1940.

To do our work we all have to read a mass of papers. Nearly all of them are far too long. This wastes time, while energy has to be spent looking for essential points.

I ask my colleagues and their staff to see to it that their reports are shorter.

1. The aim should be reports which set out the main points in a series of short, crisp paragraphs.
2. If a report relies on a detailed analysis of some complicated factors, or on statistics, these should be set out in an appendix.
3. Often the occasion is best met by submitting not a full dress report, but a reminder of headings only which can be expounded orally if needed.
4. Let us have an end to such phrases as these: "It is also important to bear in mind the following considerations." Most of these woolly phrases are mere padding, which can be left out altogether, or replaced by a single word. Let us not shrink from using the short expressive phrase, even if it is conversational.

Reports drawn up on the lines I propose may at first seem rough as compared with the flat surface of officialese jargon, but the saving in time will be great, while the discipline of setting out the real points concisely will prove an aid to clearer thinking.

Winston Churchill

First impressions

The first we see of a report is the outside. We notice how it is bound, whether it is colourful or monotone, and most important of all how big it is. For many writers size equals quality, thoroughness, attention to detail and a sense of achievement. But for the reader size simply means more time to read, understand and act on it.

Sometimes we may think it necessary to make a report look "impressive" to justify the fee we are charging for the work it represents. But mostly bigger is not necessarily better.

Titles

Like any good newspaper headline, the title should tell you what the report is going to be about. It should be to the point, but sufficiently detailed to help encourage the reader to decide to read on. To achieve this, it needs to grab the reader's attention, arouse curiosity and inform.

Not every title will follow the same pattern. Some will be quite lengthy and detailed, while others will be brief. Most will include:

- a brief description of the subject of the report;
- the date; and
- the names of the authors.

Other possible details to include in the title are:

- the person, company, or department commissioning the report;
- the name of the company, department or committee producing the report; and
- the name of the person chairing the committee, especially if the report is to be known by that person's name.

The title should be bold and clear, and if the report justifies it, on its own title page or the front cover of the report. For example:

PERFORMANCE APPRAISAL PILOT SCHEME

A report by the Management Committee on the success of the Performance Appraisal Pilot Scheme in the South West Region during the first quarter of 2016

Body

A report is a document written to provide information and ideas leading to conclusions and, if appropriate, recommendations. If a report is to fulfil its purpose it should be accurate, logically structured and pleasing to the eye. A report should then be prepared in four distinct stages.

Stage 1: Investigation

Objective - to ascertain all facts that have a bearing on the subject of the report.

- Write down the purpose of the report in one sentence and never lose sight of that purpose.
- Collect the relevant facts before you start writing.

Collecting facts is hard work and time consuming; it is however the foundation on which successful reports are based.

Stage 2: Planning

Objective - to sort through all the facts and decide in which order to present them.

- Structure reports using four main headings:
  - (a) introduction;
  - (b) body;
  - (c) conclusion; and
  - (d) recommendations.
- Collect material and decide what is and what is not important. Select material for within the body on the basis of:
  - (a) purpose and what you want to achieve;
  - (b) the readership - what they already know and what they need to know.
- Organise the material under different sections, and give each section its own subtitle. Organise these subheadings in a logical sequence, e.g.: (a) market research; (b) product development; (c) promotion; and (d) projected sales.

Stage 3: Writing

Objective - get it down on paper.

- Words, sentences and paragraphs should be short and simple.
- Use language to communicate, not to confuse.
- Use headings to grab attention and give an overview.
- "Facts are sacred, comment is free"; be clear about whether you are stating a fact or giving an opinion.
- Facts should be analysed and conclusions drawn out.
- Give illustrations a reference number (e.g. Figure 1) and ensure they are appropriately integrated and referred to in the text.

Use a simple but strong message - the aim should be to transfer all relevant information from inside your head to the reader's mind.

Stage 4: Proof reading and editing

Objective - follow the four Cs:

- **C**lear - clear enough to be understood at first reading.
- **C**oncise - all information is down to an intelligent and intelligible minimum.
- **C**omplete - all pieces of essential information have been included.
- **C**orrect - all information is accurate and verifiable.

C Clear | C Concise
C Complete | C Correct

Conclusion

The business world is full of bad, ineffective reports because business writers frequently:

- have no clear idea of the objective of the report;
- are lazy in the collection of facts;
- do not structure or format the material well; and
- use too many words.

A good report should provoke action, not confusion or inertia.

Report structure

This model represents an effective structure, which can be used in the majority of reports.

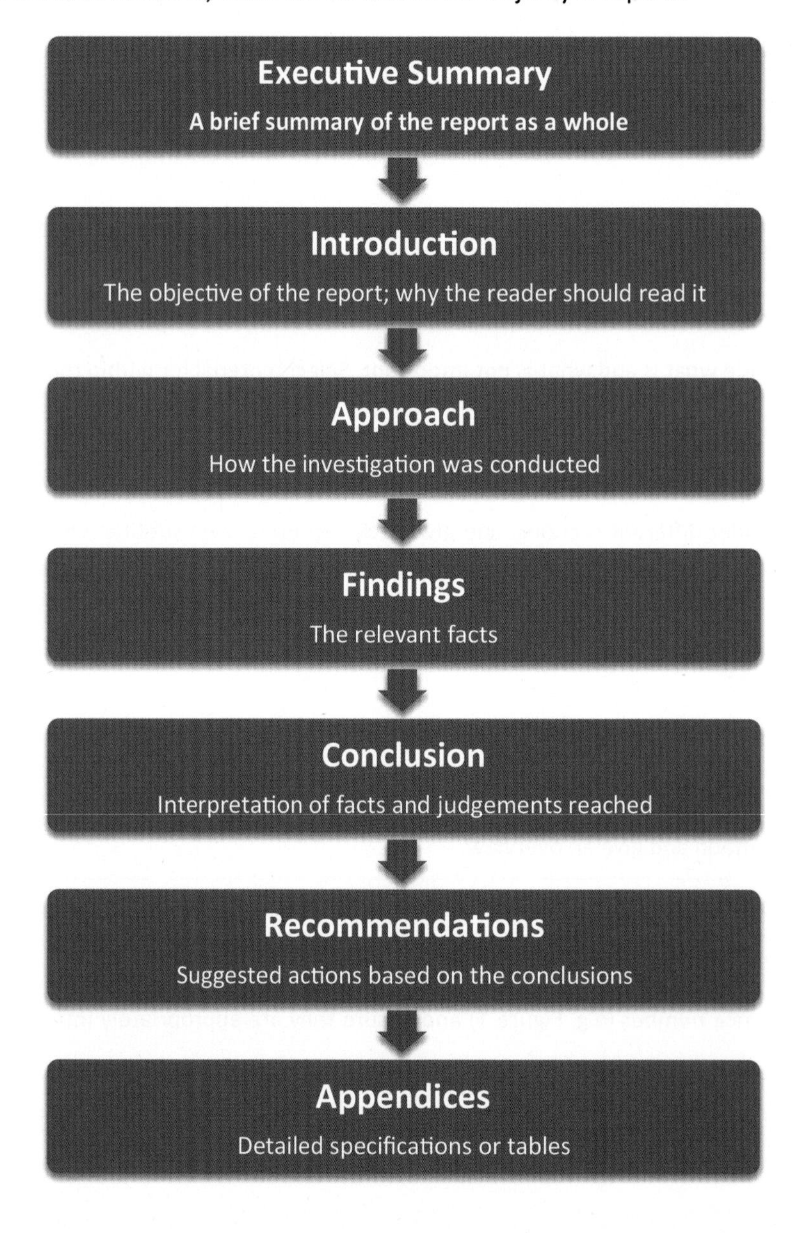

Chapter 14: Visual Aids

It is a cliché that a picture can tell a thousand words, but maybe some readers want all of the detail while other only want an overview. In that case maybe you can insert a graph or some other graphic to give the headline information, putting the thousand words into a detailed appendix for those who need it. Here are some examples of graphics commonly used in business reports.

Pie charts

- Good at showing "the big picture". The layout shows proportions very graphically, facilitating easy and effective item comparison. Pie charts generally provide a snapshot at a single point in time.
- Especially good at showing market share, performance over time, satisfaction ratings, income from different departments/ products etc.
- Not easy to discern subtle differences. A single pie chart is less effective for comparing two sets of data.

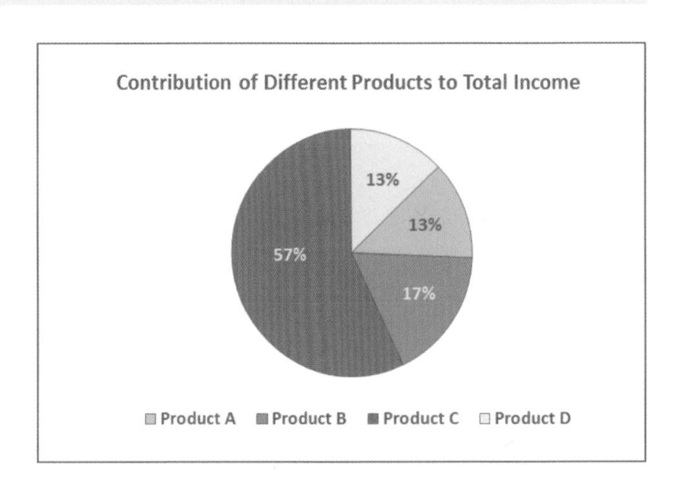

Bar charts and column charts

- Readily show trends and fluctuations in performance. Can include more components than a pie chart without the chart becoming too cluttered, as each bar/column can be broken down into smaller (coloured) segments. Bar charts and column charts generally provide snapshots over multiple periods of time.
- Especially good at showing e.g. departmental performance from one financial quarter to another, longer term growth and other trends.
- Each bar/column can only represent a snapshot at a certain point in time, whereas line graphs show more detailed progression.

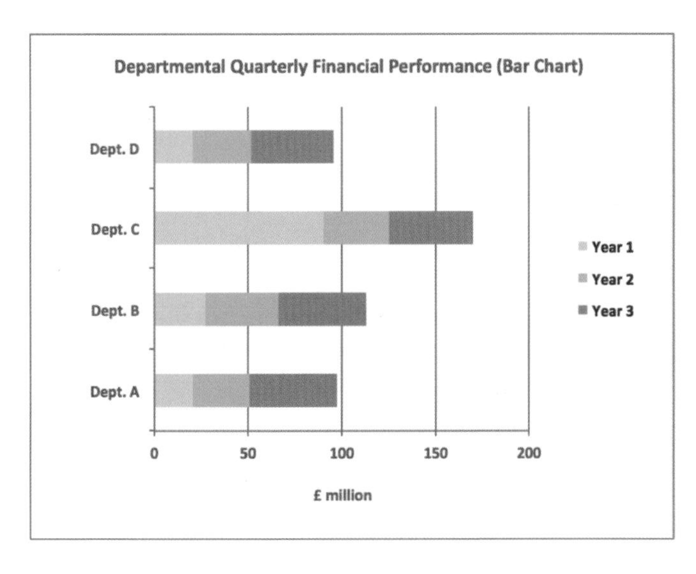

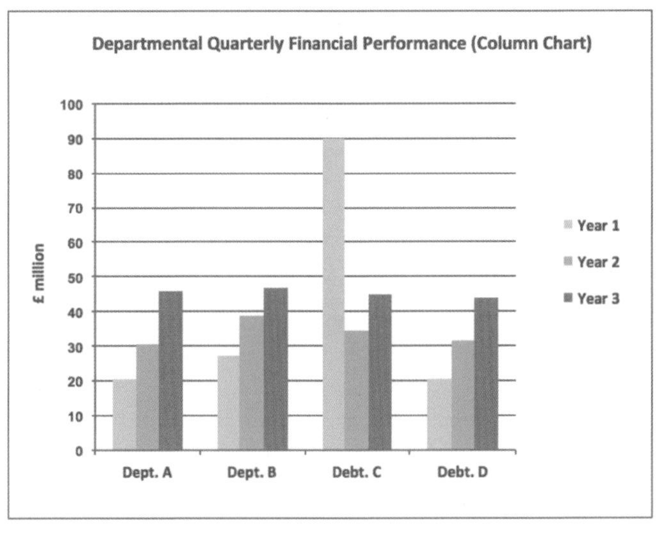

Line graphs and area graphs

- Readily show trends and fluctuations in performance, but in more detail than bar and column charts. This is because the data is not confined to particular points in time, but shows dynamic fluctuations throughout the time period.
- Especially good at showing subtle changes and cumulative data over periods of time. They also graphically illustrate longer term trends more clearly, as the lines/area shapes are not confined to the shape of a bar/column/pie.
- Line and area graphs can be difficult to read, especially if there are too many components.

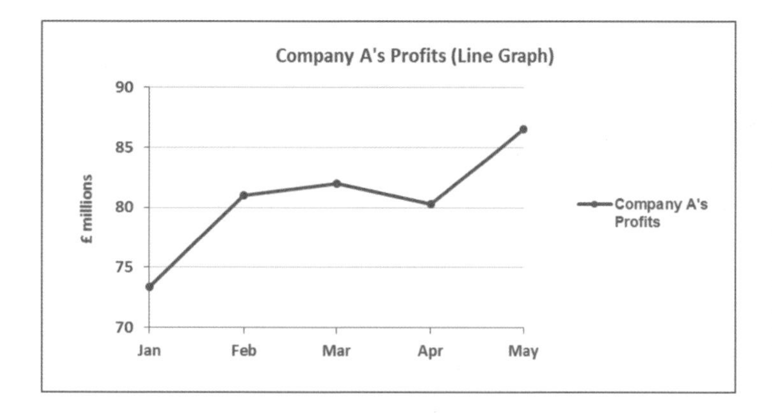

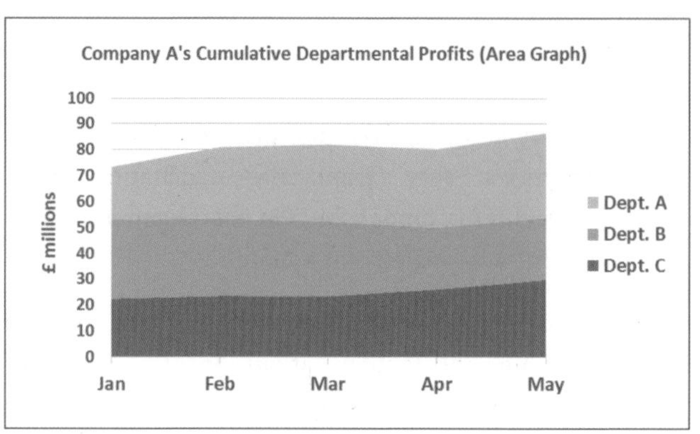

Gantt charts

- Gantt charts are named after Henry Gantt, an industrial engineer who introduced the procedure in the early 1900s. A Gantt chart shows the timescale across the top and the tasks down the side. The expected length of each task is represented by a bar which graphically represents the period in time when the task is to be completed.
- When completed the Gantt chart shows the flow of activities in sequence as well as those that can be underway at the same time. You can see the minimum total time for the project, the proper sequence of steps, and which steps can be undertaken at the same time.
- These are good for showing timelines for processes and projects and can therefore help project managers to plan for and monitor deadlines. Gantt Charts are not so good for showing detailed steps or comparing data however.

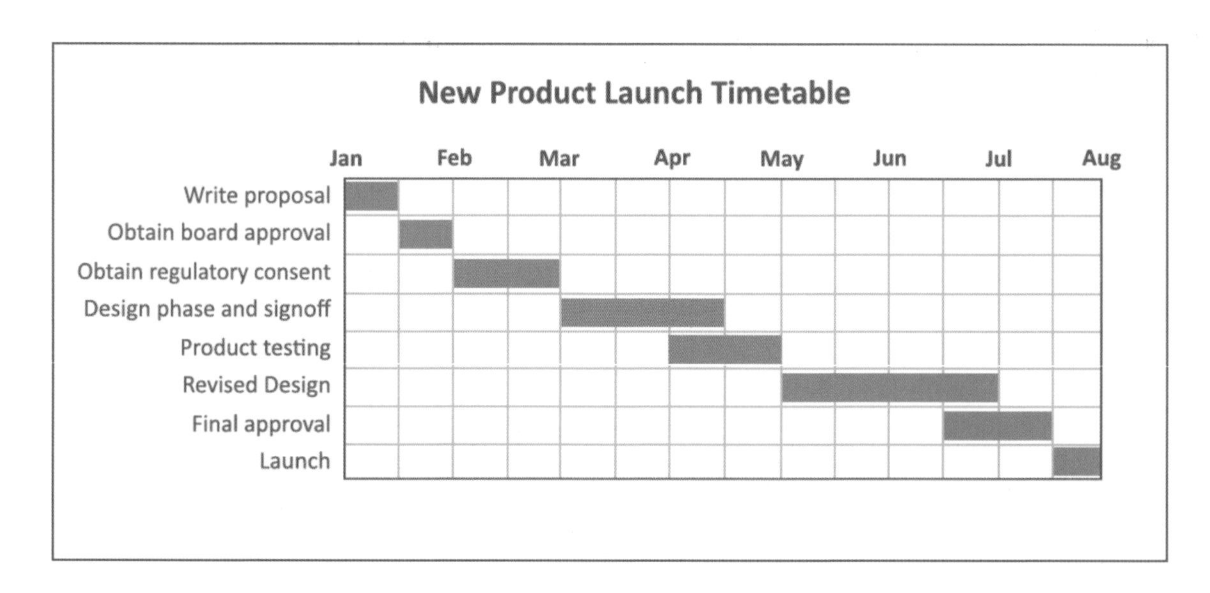

Chapter 15: Microsoft PowerPoint

Microsoft PowerPoint is a frequently used presentation tool for conferences and seminars. It can (1) add colour to a presentation and help to illustrate points more effectively; and (2) act as a trigger for the presenter if he or she loses the thread. It is arguably overused, and certainly one of the worst presentation sins is to reproduce almost every sentence on the slides. That way people end up half listening and half reading (but doing neither properly).

PowerPoint does have its place, but really it should only be used to display:

- Title pages and headings
- Photos and short video clips
- Graphs
- Flow charts
- Step-by-step instructions
- Anything else that is visually arresting

The general rule of thumb for writing on PowerPoint slides is that you should write no more than you could comfortably get onto a printed T-shirt. Make no more than three main points per slide.

Example of a bad Microsoft PowerPoint slide

Improving Profitability

Revenue: if revenues have decreased and costs have not changed, this suggests that the issue relates to revenues. Your next step should therefore be to assess whether the change is the result of a fall in the price per unit or a fall in the number of units sold. If however revenues have remained stable but costs have increased, you should then look into the different types of costs incurred by the company.

Costs: the total cost figure depends on both variable and fixed costs, so you need to determine which of the two types of costs has increased. If variable costs have increased, you must then determine if the change relates to the cost per unit or the number of units sold. If fixed costs have increased, you may have to segment the fixed costs to see whether a certain type of fixed cost has increased to an unsatisfactory extent. Remember that an increase in fixed costs may indicate investment has taken place (e.g. investment in new plant & machinery), which in the long-term could increase revenue and improve profitability (even if profitability has been negatively impacted in the short-term).

A drop in profitability may sometimes be driven by a combination of changes on both the revenues and costs sides. If this is the case, assess both costs and revenues (separately) until you find the source(s) of the problem.

There are various strategies that businesses can employ to minimise or stabilise costs. For instance: maximising economies of scale; integrating into the supply chain; outsourcing; offshoring; entering long-term contracts; using Just-In-Time Production strategies and utilising derivatives.

This is probably the worst sin committed by presenters. It is basically a reproduction of the speech. Apart from distracting the audience, this type of slide also tends to provoke the presenter into simply reading the text and therefore failing to engage the audience.

Example of a more effective Microsoft PowerPoint slide

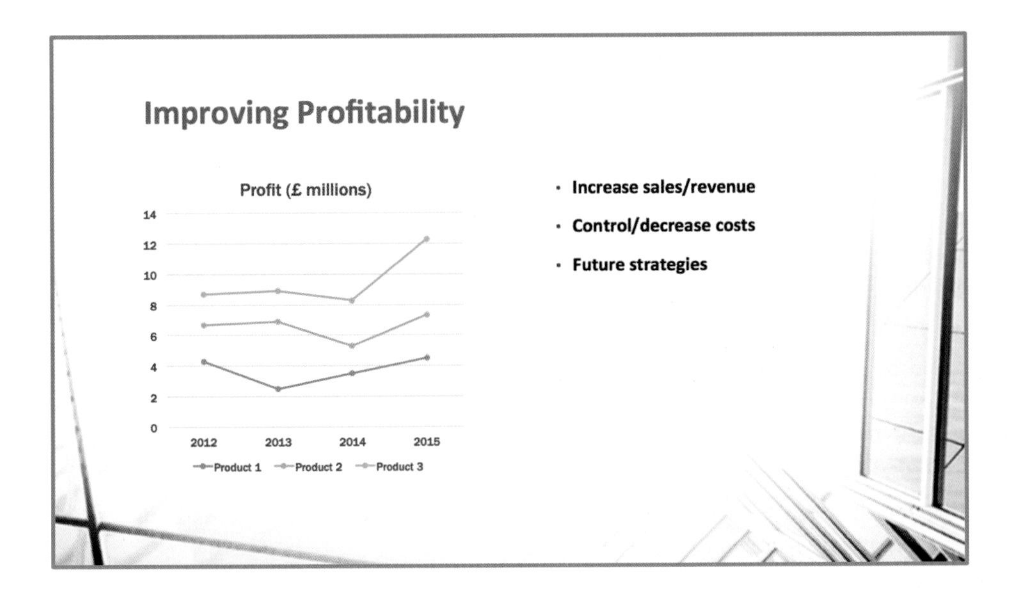

This however simply provides the headline information and a graph to illustrate the points graphically. It makes three clear points, which are likely to stay in the listeners' minds. This also allows space for the speaker to talk around the subject, to be spontaneous and to engage the audience through using a more informal tone and making more eye contact.

Chapter 16: Articles, Newsletters and Web Pages

Writing these requires you to grab the reader's attention – articles, newsletters and web pages are almost always used to try to sell products, services and ideas. This requires a particular approach, often call the pyramid writing technique. It requires us to let go of some old academic habits, because most of us are conditioned to write in an essay style, for example: (1) introduction (2) thesis (3) antithesis (4) conclusion. Instead we need to adopt a radically different structure, much more journalistic in style, which front loads the main point.

First things first

Put all the important information in the header, sub-headings and first paragraph. This should grab the reader's attention and inspire them to read on; or even if they dip out at this stage you will at least have got the main point across.

Aim to have only one main topic per page. Each page must be an "island" of information on its own so that it makes sense to the casual browser. Assume that everyone looking at your newsletter or web page has a short attention span and that he or she may be easily distracted away from your work. There are honourable exceptions, of course – like you, dear reader, if you have managed to read this far.

Presentation

Use lots of sub-headings to navigate the reader around the subject area. Try to make them explicit rather than vague, so that collectively they tell a story in their own right. "Forty years in the automotive sector" is a lot more informative than "Our experience".

Avoid italics because they are hard to read on screen. Use nice short paragraphs and follow these general guidelines: one main idea per sentence; one theme per paragraph; one topic per page. One-sentence paragraphs are fine to emphasise a crucial point, and in any event never let a paragraph stray beyond around seven sentences or fifteen lines. Too-long paragraphs simply put most readers off, so break the information down into digestible chunks.

Avoid too many hyperlinks when writing for the web – they take the reader away from your products and services. If hyperlinks are essential then try to group them together down the bottom of the page.

Example of a bad newsletter or web page

WEEKLY NEWSLETTER

Dangerous buildings and structures

Owners of buildings have a responsibility to deal with dangers and emergencies as they occur. Buildings may gradually deteriorate through old age long-term settlement, or there may be sudden outside events like storms, explosions, fire or accidents. All buildings that appear to be dangerous should be dealt with as expeditiously as possible.

If a building appears to be immediately dangerous, then NW3 Property Maintenance Services can assist with the building's immediate evacuation and take all necessary action to protect the public and adjoining properties. This could include temporary road closures, barricading, shoring up of walls, scaffolding, repairs and emergency demolition.

If a building is not immediately dangerous, the owner may still receive a notice from the local authority requiring it to be made safe within a specified time, and if this is not done the local authority has the statutory power to carry out all appropriate remedial works to make it safe and to recover all reasonable costs from the owner.

NW3 Property Maintenance Services therefore offer an invaluable service to all institutional landlords and property owners.

This is not written with the reader in mind, and the lack of aids to readability aids like headings makes it somewhat impenetrable.

Example of a more effective newsletter or webpage

WEEKLY NEWSLETTER

Dangerous buildings and structures

NW3 Property Maintenance Services offer an invaluable service to all institutional landlords and property owners when faced with dangers and emergencies. Buildings may gradually deteriorate through old age long-term settlement, or there may be sudden outside events like storms, explosions, fire or accidents. All buildings that appear to be dangerous should be dealt with as quickly as possible.

Emergency measures

If a building appears to be immediately dangerous, then NW3 Property Maintenance Services can assist with the building's immediate evacuation and take all necessary action to protect the public and adjoining properties. This could include temporary road closures, barricading, shoring up of walls, scaffolding, repairs and emergency demolition.

Local authority powers

If a building is not immediately dangerous, the owner may still receive a notice from the local authority requiring it to be made safe within a set time. If this is not done the local authority has the statutory power to carry out remedial works to make it safe and to recover all reasonable costs from the owner. It is always cheaper to deal proactively with these matters, though, which is where we can help.

Contact details line up properly

Call us on 07912 249391 or email
nw3@propertymaintenance.com

Chapter 17: Meeting Notes

Taking notes of meetings is probably one of the least enjoyable writing tasks in business life. Many people get writer's cramp by trying to take a verbatim note, which is an endeavour that is almost certainly doomed to failure. If you want a word-for-word note then you should put a recorder in the room and have a transcript typed up afterwards. Instead focus on the essential ABC:

- Actions – who has agreed to do what?
- Balance – reflect the different viewpoints that may have been aired in the room.
- Clarity – use plain English to avoid ambiguity.

The main focus on meeting notes should therefore be to reflect the broad ideas, discussion points and decisions from the meeting. The rules of plain English are certainly helpful here for presenting the notes. It is also a good idea to dictate or type the notes up as soon as possible after the meeting because the best shorthand can start to lose meaning after 24 hours.

Practical steps

1. Before the meeting

- Read the agenda.
- Talk to the chairperson about what format (s)he would like the minutes in, whether you can interrupt etc.
- Talk to others, e.g. experts whose opinions are particularly important, speakers whose contributions may need clarifying.
- Consider who will be attending the meeting, and what its overall objective will be.

2. During the meeting

- Sit in a suitable place.
- Find out who is who – look at the attendance list or place cards, or if necessary ask.
- Clarify anything you do not understand – interrupt if you can, or speak to people afterwards.
- Take notes – use plain English to write as economically as possible, and remember to focus on the message rather than the words used. Remember to record actions and actors in particular.
- Do not get obsessed with figures and statistics – if necessary you can add these later.

3. After the meeting

- Write up your notes as soon as possible.
- Follow agreed procedures about getting the minutes approved and circulated.

Shorthand for meeting notes

Here are some commons useful abbreviations to use in your handwritten notes only. Obviously the full meeting notes need to feature proper words and sentences.

- "Assoc" for association
- "Bkgd" for background
- "Mvmt" for movement
- "Gvt" for government
- "E.g." / "Etc" / "I.e."
- "%" – but write "per cent" in longhand notes
- "v." for versus in legal case names

Many organisations have a particular style for meeting notes. Some, for example, have a right hand column for initials of people who have to carry out the action points. There is no absolute format, but the following set of notes is fairly typical. Everyone has their own shorthand so try to extend this list as much as possible. A final tip is to get a good thick-barrelled pen, preferably with a rubber grip. This will minimise writer's cramp.

Good example of meeting notes

Higher School Parents Association (HSPA)

Minutes of a Committee Meeting held at 59 Litchfield Way, NW12 on 19th November 2017

Present: Susan Dodds, Ricardo Santos, Ernest Pickles, Emma Emmanuel, Moira Jones (Chair), Helen Howes, John Trimbos

Apologies: Richard Auchinleck, Mark Hughes, Deborah Meades

Gifts to School

Resolutions:

- HSPA would give £500 to each of the Senior, Middle and Junior School libraries; HSPA would also give £500 to the language library.
- HSPA would give approximately £1,250 to the drama department for a computerised lighting deck.
- HSPA would make a £40 contribution to food and drink for all future committee meetings this year.

Moira reported that the Headmaster was looking into playground equipment for the Senior/Middle School playground. He asked HSPA to look at the website www.snuggleplay.co.uk and consider whether the surplus funds (£7,500), may be put towards play equipment (costing approx. £10,500).

The school is still thinking about building a play area on top of the sports hall (estimated cost £400,000 + fees), but would need planning permission.

Ricardo asked if HSPA money could be spent on repairing seatbelts on the school minibus. Moira reported that the school was buying a new minibus in the near future so this would be unnecessary.

Uniform

The committee members agreed that uniform was becoming increasingly difficult to get from major department stores. Supply levels are appalling and orders take weeks to materialise, if at all. Moira has been talking to the school about changing suppliers, and meetings are planned with two smaller specialist suppliers. A small committee of parents and teachers will be formed.

Discussion on the future role of the HSPA

The committee discussed the following questions, although there is no need for any immediate decisions.

- Should our primary objective be to foster fellowship between the school and parents?
- Should fundraising be a primary objective? And if so should it be for charity or gifts to the school or both, as at present
- Should a further objective be increased involvement of the parents by utilising their skills in giving regular, informal talks to the boys etc.?
- Should we incorporate all of the above and carry on much as we are now?

Much discussion took place about these questions. Also, should HSPA have its own chosen charity and if it did should it be linked to the school? Should HSPA have a clearer strategy in the choice of charity and in particular a charity which is relevant to the boys?

These topics are to be discussed further at forthcoming committee meetings. The committee members decided to consider these ideas and to canvass views from other parents in the meantime.

Fun Events

The committee decided to look into more fun social activities for the boys and parents e.g. firework party, year 8 disco, Halloween party and any other ideas that may come up. HSPA could do more to encourage parents to feel more involved with the school. A sub-committee was formed to research such events, comprising Ricardo Santos, Ernest Pickles and Emma Emmanuel.

Next meeting

7.30pm, Monday 14th January 2018 at 59 Litchfield Way, NW12

A little light relief...

Taken from a set of meeting notes: "The committee requires a list of our staff, broken down by age and sex."

Chapter 18: CVs and Cover Letters

There is no objectively "correct" way in which to structure curricula vitae (CVs) and cover letters. Different firms in different industries will have different preferences. It is worth undertaking additional research in order to ascertain exactly what the firm you are applying to expects. This section simply provides some basic pointers that you may want to consider. Avoid lying or overly embellishing the truth. You risk getting caught out, which in turn will reflect negatively upon your character and may cause the firm to question all the other statements you have made. Avoid being too generic and tailor your application to the particular role/firm in question.

CVs

Bear in mind that whilst a majority of financial services firms tend to expect one page CVs, some (especially law firms) prefer two page CVs. Some firms do not request CVs at all. Before starting to draft your CV, check what the firm to which you are applying expects and perhaps utilise your network to source examples of CVs that have helped applicants in the past to secure interviews. CVs provide an insight into your past experiences and achievements and evidence your writing style, your ability to distil information into short, concise sentences, your skill at structuring documents and your attention to detail. Do not be afraid to include more interesting or unique interests and experiences if you have space, as this can help you to stand out.

Avoid spelling and grammatical mistakes (and ask people to proof read your CV for you). Make sure your headings, dates, bullet points and font are in a consistent format and properly aligned. Your layout should look professional: avoid the use of flowery borders, bright colours and cartoon images (it happens!). Make sure the structure is clear and really outlines your experiences and achievements, even on a quick skim. Recruiters are unlikely to pour over your CV for long (evidence suggests that on the first look through a CV, employers give it attention for no more than 30 seconds). You could split your CV into sections, including for instance:

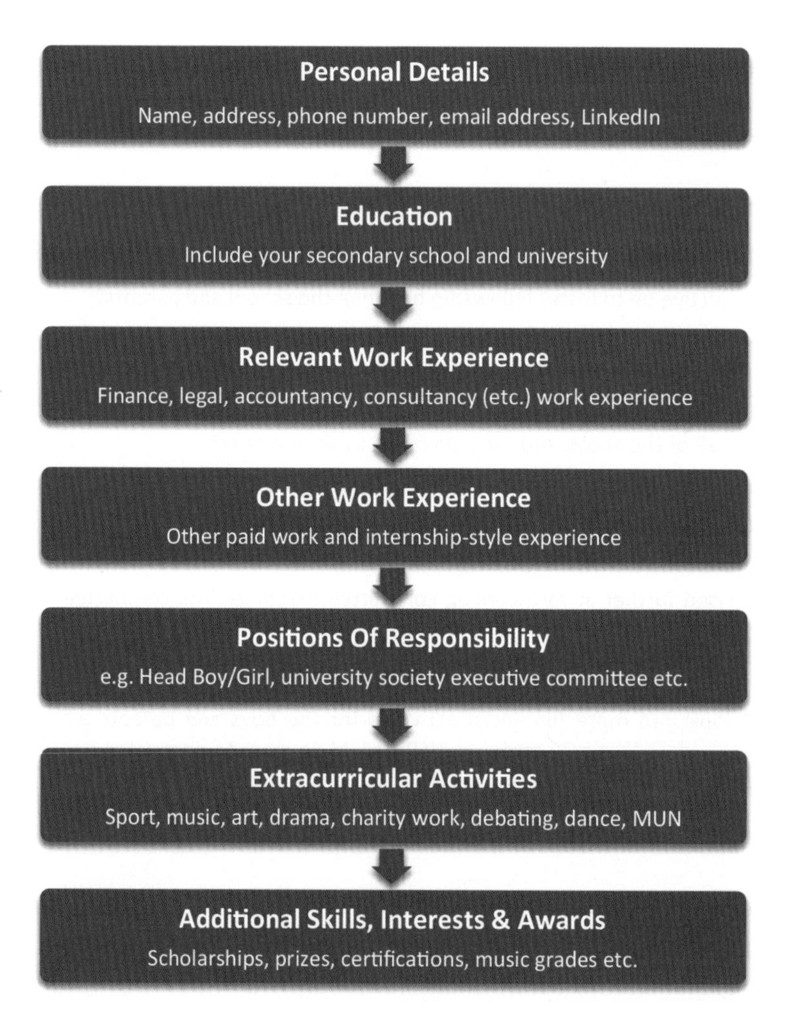

Use space wisely, especially if your CV is only one page long. Filling the page with large headings and including bullet points that contain only a couple of words could suggest you have little to say about yourself. Conversely, keep your sentences concise and to the point and avoid repetition.

Cover letters

As with CVs, there is no objectively correct way in which to structure cover letters. Some firms may set word or character limits. Others may simply ask you to attach a separate document. Cover letters for established graduate schemes at large City firms should probably include an overview of your reasons for making the application and an insight into why you believe you are a suitable candidate. Cover letters for other types of roles may require greater emphasis on your competencies. Research into what is expected for the particular role for which you are applying.

Bear in mind that making speculative applications for casual work experience can call for a very different technique than that required when making full-time job applications. For example, if you are applying for experience at a small high street firm, you will not necessarily need to spend ages distinguishing it from similar employers in the same street. Approach your application from the basis of "what I can do for you" rather than "what you can do for me".

Cover letters should be fairly concise (usually one page) and should be well written (accurate spelling and grammar) with a strong structure. After all, this may well provide the firm with its first impression of the standard of work that you are able to deliver. Whilst drafting your cover letter, using temporary headings can help to ensure you maintain a clear structure.

Example cover letter structure

Mr/Mrs Your Name
Your Address
Your Phone Number
Your Email Address

Mr/Mrs Name Of Recruiter

Employer's Name
Employer's Address

Date

1. **Salutation (Dear...)**
   - Try to find the name of the specific person that will be receiving your application. This shows good research and professionalism. Otherwise, use "Dear Sir/Madam".
2. **Heading**
   - Summarise to purpose of the letter using a bold heading between the salutation and the introduction, e.g. **'Summer Internship Application'**.
3. **Introduction**
   - State the role/opportunity for which you are applying.
4. **State your reasons for applying for the job**
   - Tell the story of how your interest in your chosen career has developed.
5. **State your reasons for applying to the particular firm**
   - Do not give generic reasons for applying to that firm that merely reflect a quick skim of the firm's marketing materials. Think of legitimate ways to differentiate the firm and more importantly, relate these elements back to you in order to convince recruiters that these factors genuinely appeal.
6. **Explain why you believe that you are a suitable candidate**
   - Relate your skills to the competencies required for the role in question and briefly explain how your strengths and experiences will add value/be advantageous to the organisation.
7. **Conclusion**
   - You could thank the reader for considering your application before signing off. Sign off with "Yours sincerely" if you know the name of the reader, or "Yours faithfully" if you do not.

More than any other type of correspondence, cover letters should be seriously customised to suit the opportunity and recipient. Do not assume the above structure should always be followed.

In Conclusion...

Seven deadly sins

We started this book with seven deadly sins of writing. Hopefully now you will be well equipped to avoid these (unless you have skipped straight to the conclusion). To reiterate, these are:

1. Writing for yourself rather than for the reader
2. Putting up barriers between you and your readership
3. Failing to observe ABC (Accuracy, Brevity, Clarity)
4. Failing to write for a global audience
5. Using too many abbreviations or jargon
6. Using too many hyperlinks
7. Failing to proof read and check the finished work

Ten commandments

On a more positive note here are ten commandments to follow. For no apparent reason they all begin with P, so if you are secular in nature just follow the ten Ps:

1. **P**lan your work before you launch into the word-for-word writing to determine the right tone, level and structure. As they say in the army: "If you fail to plan, you plan to fail."

2. **P**unctuate all your work properly, even the briefest email. Everything you send out reflects on you and your organisation.

3. **P**ersuade – much business writing is intended to persuade people to your point of view; so maximise the impact of your writing through using short, punchy sentences and base verbs.

4. **P**arts of speech – this term of art indicates the various components of a sentence, i.e. nouns, verbs, adjectives etc. Knowledge of parts of speech will help you write better, clearer sentences.

5. **P**rune out any unnecessary/excess words so no one misunderstands you.

6. **P**eruse the text – does it flow and have a mixture of longer and shorter sentences and paragraphs?

7. **P**oliteness – in all business correspondence you cannot be criticised for being a bit too formal or polite.

8. **P**resentation – do not forget aids to readability like headings, bullet points and strategic page breaks.

9. **P**ictures – if a picture tells a thousand words then maybe use one instead; or use both words and a picture, but move the thousand words into an appendix and give more casual readers the headline information only.

10. **P**roof read everything and do not trust your computer too much.

And always...

Now put this book in your desk drawer at work and when no one is looking, give it a quick check whenever you are about to work on or send out an important document. We will not tell anyone. Finally, good luck and all the best.

John Trimbos and Jake Schogger.